SEX EDUCATION

a guide to life

the no-nonsense sex education you always wanted

Running Press Teens
Hachette Book Group
1290 Avenue of the Americas,
New York, NY 10104
www.runningpress.com/rpkids
@RP_Kids

Printed in China

Originally published in 2021 by Wren & Rook in Great Britain
First U.S. Edition: January 2022

Published by Running Press Teens, an imprint of Perseus Books, LLC, a subsidiary of Hachette Book Group, Inc. The Running Press Teens name and logo is a trademark of the Hachette Book Group.

The Hachette Speakers Bureau provides a wide range of authors for speaking events. To find out more, go to www.hachettespeakersbureau.com or call (866) 376-6591.

The publisher is not responsible for websites (or their content) that are not owned by the publisher.

Additional illustrations by Fionna Fernandes.
Additional images supplied by Shutterstock.
Written with Jordan Paramor.

Library of Congress Control Number: 2021941965

ISBNs: 978-0-7624-8030-2 (paperback), 978-0-7624-8031-9 (ebook)

RDS

10 9 8 7 6 5 4 3 2 1

SEX EDUCATION

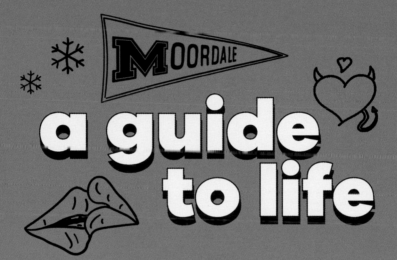

MOORDALE

a guide to life

the no-nonsense sex education you always wanted

Foreword by series creator
Laurie Nunn

RP | TEENS
PHILADELPHIA

CONTENTS

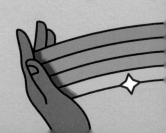

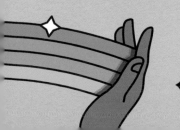

FOREWORD

Secondary school was a pretty uncomfortable experience for me. At sixteen years old, I was painfully awkward, had thick braces on my teeth, wore glasses and suffered from chronic backne (acne of the back). Along with an obsession with musical theatre and writing *Lord of the Rings* fan-fiction, I felt like I was doomed to never fit in. Like many a nerdy teen before me, I turned to YA films and TV shows as a way to escape my reality. I lived vicariously through the characters of *Dawson's Creek, The OC* and *Ten Things I Hate About You*. Watching them making friends, falling in love and having sex made me feel less alone. In these teenage universes, the bullies always got their comeuppance, the geeks always succeeded and the invisible girls always got the boy of their dreams. As someone who was never invited to the dance or picked for the sports team, and still hadn't been kissed, these stories made me feel seen.

I've carried this love of the teen genre into my adult life. If I'm ever feeling low, I'll put on a nineties teen rom-com and instantly feel better. So, when I started writing for TV I knew it was a teenage world I wanted to inhabit, and *Sex Education* was the perfect vehicle to let my inner sixteen-year-old-invisible-girl fly. I wanted to create a show that felt warm and uplifting, where characters were kind to each other and vulnerability was considered brave. I also wanted the series to be a call for better communication and an antidote to the inadequate information most of us were taught about sex and relationships at school.

FREE SEX Advice

My memories of sex and relationships education at secondary school mostly center around fear and shame. The main message I was given was that sex was a terrifying act that would either leave me pregnant or with an itchy, STI-ridden vagina . . . or both! I was given zero information about my body, sexuality, desire or agency as a young woman, and even less about the wants and needs of people with identities different to my own. Sadly, this dire sex and relationships education is a common experience for many people and is something that can leave emotional scars. Which is why it has been heartwarming to see the response young people have had to *Sex Education* and to witness the conversations about consent, body positivity, LGBTQI+ issues and female pleasure it has provoked.

But there are always more questions that need answering and only so much information the show can provide, which is why I was so excited when I heard about *Sex Education: A Guide to Life*. This book is the kind of guide I needed when I was sixteen and looking for insightful, frank and non-judgmental information about how to navigate the brand-new world of sex. Each chapter has been overseen by brilliant, smart and diverse sex educators, and covers everything from pubic hair to getting over heartbreak. And there's some sage advice from Moordale's finest along the way. Like the show, this book celebrates the messy reality of being a teenager and encourages people to talk about the things we're scared of and to ask for help when we need it. Whether you're a nerd, invisible or just misunderstood, I hope you learn something from this book and that it makes you feel a little less alone and a little more seen.

Laurie Nunn, creator of *Sex Education*

LET'S TALK ABOUT SEX

Welcome, one and all,

Have you ever found yourself questioning relationships or feeling confused about sex or identity? Maybe you're looking for answers to all those burning friendship, mental health and happiness questions you're too afraid to ask? Well, you're not alone; just ask the students of Moordale.

With so much conflicting information out there, navigating the modern world can feel like a minefield. Especially when, even in this day and age, sex can still be seen as something that's embarrassing to talk about. Stigma around these topics only leads to worry, anxiety and shame. But there is *nothing* to be ashamed of when it comes to mental and physical well-being.

So much sex and relationship information is outdated, confusing or doesn't reflect the vast spectrum of people's personal experiences, and the students of Moordale know firsthand how bad it can be (their sex-ed classes are case in point). The students were crying out for their old-fashioned and rather clueless sex and relationships education to be updated, and this book aims to answer all their questions and more.

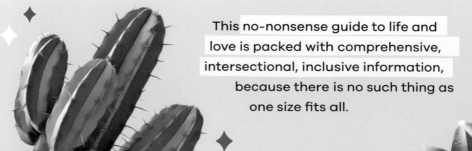

This no-nonsense guide to life and love is packed with comprehensive, intersectional, inclusive information, because there is no such thing as one size fits all.

Everyone has the right to feel empowered and informed, and that's why a doctor and two professional sex educators have consulted on this indispensable guide to give you the tools to develop a healthy relationship with sex and emotions, and to discover what feels right for you.

And on top of that, the sex, love and life experiences of Otis and his friends at Moordale are included throughout the book – maybe they can teach you a thing or two as well.

So dive in, and start talking, shouting and maybe even screaming about

S-e-x!

Ola

MOORDALE SECONDARY

Lily

Eric

Aimee

Jackson

Adam

Otis

Maeve

Ruby

Anwar & Olivia

ON **REPORT**

Someone has got their hands on some of the students' files. What does new Headteacher, Hope, really think of Otis and his friends? Read on . . .

 SCHOOL FILES: CONFIDENTIAL

THE NERDY ONE: **OTIS MILBURN**

- Ran a sex clinic under the pretence of being helpful – does he just want to find out about other people's sex lives?
- Used to blend into the background until he started the sex clinic and brought up all this sex education nonsense.

THE CONFLICTED JOCK: **JACKSON MARCHETTI**

- Former Head Boy. Was the pride of Moordale before he "found" himself and went off the rails.
- Sensitive but smart. There's still a chance he can be guided back onto the right path.

THE ECCENTRIC ONE: **LILY IGLEHART**

- Alien-obsessed and in her own world most of the time.
- She was the "brains" behind the school production of *Romeo and Juliet*. Inappropriate!

THE DITZY ONE: **AIMEE GIBBS**

- Sweet but spaced out – perhaps not the most academically minded.
- Had a horrible sexual assault experience with a man on a bus so extra support may be needed. *NB: avoid any home-baked goods.

THE FRIENDLY ONE: **ERIC EFFIONG**

- Always happy and appears to be liked by everyone.
- Needs to concentrate more on his schoolwork and less on his love life and fashion choices.

THE SUPER SMART ONE: **VIVIENNE ODESANYA**

- Far too clever for her own good. Extremely driven and knows what she wants.
- Scarily focused but perhaps lacking in self-confidence.

THE DISRUPTIVE ONE: **ADAM GROFF**

- Son of former Headteacher, Mr. Groff.
- Previously very angry and difficult to deal with.
- Appears to finally want to get an education. Time will tell if he goes back to his old ways.

THE CURIOUS ONE: **OLA NYMAN**

- Always direct and to the point. Open to new experiences – see relationship with fellow student, Lily.
- Very level-headed and hardworking but has had some difficulties adapting to her new living arrangements. May need some extra support at times.

THE UNTOUCHABLES: **ANWAR BAKSHI, OLIVIA ANAND, RUBY MATTHEWS**

- ⊗ These three come as a pack – Ruby is a leader while the others follow.
- ⊗ They are untouchable because they are the popular group and think they are much better than everyone else.
- ⊗ Ruby's recent relationship with Otis could threaten the group dynamics – keep a close eye on the situation.

THE SCARY ONE: **MAEVE WILEY**

- ⊗ Can come across as unapproachable, sometimes a bit too smart for her own good.
- ⊗ Highly intelligent and will go far if she gets the right breaks. Could be the first ex-Moordale student to become Prime Minister?

THE OUTSPOKEN ONE: **CAL BOWMAN**

- ⊗ Asks to be referred to as they/them. Part of the group of skater kids at Moordale.
- ⊗ Despite best efforts, will not conform to new uniform rules. Potential to cause trouble.

THE COOL ONE: **RAHIM HARRAK**

- ⊗ Can come across as petulant and brooding.
- ⊗ Is always reading poetry, but it would be nice to see him smile a bit more.

FRIENDSHIP AND WHY IT MATTERS

Good friends are an invaluable part of life. Knowing that you have amazing people to share experiences with, chat to and lean on when times get tough can mean the world.

Some people may only be in your life for a short time, while other friendships might last for years. As people grow and change, so do some friendships, and it's natural for these relationships to shift during your life. There may be some friends you slowly lose a connection with and never rebuild, while others you may not see for months or even years, but when you do it all falls back into place.

Building a strong friendship takes time and effort, and there may well be ups and downs to navigate. As with any relationship, communication is king!

WHAT MAKES A GOOD FRIEND?

Friendships are all about quality rather than quantity. Good friends are there to lift you up, enhance your life and make you feel great. They are people you can have fun and go on adventures with, and talk through the night about anything and everything.

When you need someone to rely on, keep your secrets and turn to if times are tough, a good friend comes into their own. They are honest (but not hurtfully so), supportive (but will gently tell you if they think your outfit is hideous) and help you discover more about who you are.

Friendships can sometimes come from unexpected places. You don't always need to have tons in common with someone to be their friend. Just because your friend only listens to death metal and you're a Taylor Swift fan doesn't mean you can't be good friends. Friendship is about more than sharing interests; it's about having a connection, being able to laugh together and, more importantly, being able to trust each other.

When I started working with Adam at the shop, he had a tough exterior but I sensed that he had so much more to him and I really wanted to get to know him better. Although it seemed we had nothing in common, simply being nice helped him to slowly open up to me. I realized that his tough exterior was just for show and he was actually really unhappy and unsure of himself. By being kind and listening to him when no one else did, I gained a pretty cool new friend. And it turns out we do have some things in common after all!

OLA

You don't have to be glued to someone's side and being a good friend isn't about counting how many hours you spend together. Sometimes you can have amazing connections with a person you never even really considered to be a friend. What's more important is being there when someone needs you.

I've always been happy being myself, even if it's a bit different. I never felt like I needed to change to fit in with other people. But everything with Hope at school made me question how I express myself and really knocked my confidence. I suddenly felt like I needed to try and be less, well, me. It was actually Otis who helped me to see that I should never compromise on who I am and what I like. We aren't exactly close, so I would never have expected him to be the one that helped me out. But I guess what he said was true; you don't need to hang out with someone 24/7 to be friends.

LILY

> *When you're young you think that everybody out there really, really gets you. But, you know, only a handful of them do.*
> **REMI**

I'VE GOT **YOUR BACK**

What's one of the most important things you can do as a friend? Having your friends' backs, supporting them and standing up for them when they need it most has got to be up there.

It's all too common for people to be unkind, especially with the anonymity of the internet. But if you see or hear someone being mean or making fun of another person, **call them out**. It's easy to ignore comments and feel like you don't want to get involved, but if people feel like they can get away with saying hurtful things, when will they stop? If you don't feel comfortable speaking to them directly, you could speak to a teacher or trusted adult or ask for support from other friends. If it's happening over social media, you can report abusive behavior.

This is especially important when it comes to marginalized groups. Abuse towards people based on race, identity, sexuality or disability happens all the time and they often receive much less support when it is reported. Everyone has a part to play and something that may seem small, like calling out a comment or offering a friendly word, can make all the difference to someone who might feel like they are going through it alone.

Otis and I always go and see Hedwig and the Angry Inch *on my birthday – we get dressed up and have the best time. When he didn't show because he was too busy with Vagina-gate, I was so upset he had let me down. But what made it even worse was that by leaving me alone he put me in a really vulnerable position. I ended up being the victim of a hate crime thanks to some small-minded idiots and it took me a while to regain my confidence. Otis didn't think about my safety and that is what hurt the most.*

ERIC

FREN**EMIES**

When it comes to friendships, not all of them are healthy. But what makes someone a crap friend? There are lots of things, but some of the most common are someone who:

✖ Is unkind to you

✖ Talks about you behind your back

✖ Always puts their feelings before yours

✖ Puts you down

✖ Drops you when someone better comes along

If someone is treating you in any way that makes you feel bad about yourself, it's not OK. **You deserve better.**

Don't be afraid to let go of friendships that aren't working for you. Toxic friendships can seriously affect your mental health (read chapter ten for more on this), so it's essential that you distance yourself from anyone who has a negative effect on how you feel. By calling time on a destructive relationship, you can also make space for someone better to come along who will appreciate being sent fifty "hilarious" cat TikToks every day.

It's common to want to feel cool or popular, but that doesn't mean you have to be shallow or treat people unkindly. Do you really want to hang out with the Mean Girls? It may seem like a great idea at first (who doesn't like the idea of being part of the A-list?), but fall-outs and bitching behind people's backs soon become wearing.

Sending a picture of Ruby's vagina to the entire school was really wrong. She had pushed me to my limit and I couldn't take it any more, but there's never an excuse for sending images without consent. I was too scared to stand up to her in person, and I was so angry it felt like my only option. But now I realize that hurting someone else is not the way to express my feelings. I'd always try and talk it out now.
OLIVIA

Being popular and being respected are two very different things. Some people may be revered for being good at sport or always looking trendy and be constantly surrounded by people, but when the chips are down they may not have anyone to call. At the end of the day, don't you want to know that if something goes down you'll have friends who've got your back, rather than dropping you like last week's filter?

SQUAD **GOALS**

Don't panic if you don't feel like you've found your tribe yet. It's not always easy for everyone to make friends, and it's common to feel lonely sometimes. Some people might meet their BFFs at elementary school, some people find them online and some people might not make good friends until much later in life. There's nothing wrong with you if you don't have a big group of friends; everyone is different. If you struggle to make new friends, you could try connecting with people who have similar interests, either online or in person.

If you know you have a handful of people you can count on and who will always have your back, you're doing well, but some people are happy just having one BFF. Look at Maeve and Aimee. They've got plenty of friends and people that they can hang around with, but in a crisis, they're always there for each other and are a solid unit of two.

BFFs!

FRIENDS BEFORE **DATES**

When you spend a lot of time with the same friend(s), the chances are you will meet a lot of the same people, and some of those people may be hot. So, what happens if you both find yourselves lusting over the same potential partner or you start falling for a friend's ex?

The first thing you need to do is talk it over and come to an arrangement you are both happy with. Some good questions to consider:

Would you feel like you're in competition with your friend?

If the person in question made a move, how would your friend feel?

Are you sure it wouldn't eventually come between you, no matter how hard you try?

If you got together, would it be awkward to hang out as a group?

Would your friend still be cool if they have to see you making out on a night out?

In these situations you're going to have to be totally honest with your friend. The important thing here is to speak up. Of course we all want our friends to be happy, but do we want that to affect our friendship long term? There is no point in being noble now and furious later.

What if you thought you'd be cool with it and then find you're seething with jealousy later? It may be that your feelings fade, or perhaps you're even jealous of losing your friend to someone else. Whatever it may be, the best thing to do is talk it out and be honest with your friend.

> *Who needs a friend when you have a boyfriend?*
> **ERIC**

If in doubt, follow the advice in these really well-thought-out rhymes:

Chicks before dicks

Pals before gals

ovaries before brovaries

Dongs before thongs

Fries before guys

Friends before hens

(because fries need love, too)

SPACE IS **ACE**

There is nothing wrong with having the odd argument or disagreement with friends. We can be so close to some of our friends that they feel like family and sometimes the closer you are, the easier it is to fall out. But in every relationship there has to be a level of respect, so don't fall into the trap of taking people for granted and thinking you can get away with saying whatever you want. Everyone has their limits and sometimes when you cross a line, there's no going back.

Honesty is the best policy. A lot of the time, people are more hurt by the feeling they've been lied to than the actual cause of the argument.

I was livid when I found out that Aimee's mum had paid for me to go on the French trip and we had a big row. I know she thought she had done the right thing but it was so embarrassing to be seen like I needed charity. I was so annoyed, and I could tell Aimee was pretty angry too, so the best thing to do was give each other space to cool off before we even thought about making amends. If we'd tried to sort it then and there, I think we would have ended up having another argument.

MAEVE

> *Apologizing isn't just social etiquette, it's a hugely important human ritual that brings relationships together and helps people to move forwards.*
> **JEAN**

It's very easy to fall into a "poor me" trap, or to blame the other person following a fight. Emotions are heightened, and your body has gone into fight or flight mode so your nervous system is screaming at you, meaning you're not always able to think calmly or rationally.

Taking time away from the person you've argued with allows you to process what was said, and sometimes (as annoying as it can be) it also gives you the chance to realize that maybe the other person wasn't *totally* to blame, and you may both need to take some responsibility.

IT'S OK NOT TO **LIKE EVERYONE**

In this huge and varied world not everyone is going to get along. Humans are strange and complex creatures; people have different interests, some personalities just don't gel and some people project their insecurities onto others, making it difficult to be friends with them.

It's totally fine to not get along with someone, but that doesn't give you the right to be a dick to them. You have to just live and let live. Even sworn enemies Rahim and Adam manage to be civil to each other most of the time, and Rahim almost – *almost* – compliments Adam when he tells him,

You're not as unremarkable as I thought.

Way to make someone feel good about themselves, Rahim.

Don't take it to heart if you're not someone's cup of tea either. You don't need to be liked by everyone to be good enough. You're good enough already. Trying to get validation from other people's opinions of you is never going to lead to happiness. The only opinions that *really* matter are yours and the ones of the people that you know and love.

OVERHEARD **MOORDALE**

Everybody's either thinking about SHAGGING, about to SHAG, or actually SHAGGING.
ERIC

I think I know where the hymen is, but thanks.
MAEVE

You're my friend. I love you like a friend.
OLA

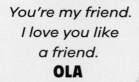

You'll feel him throbbing in your hand like a volcano about to erupt.
JEAN

We all have flaws, and our bodies do things we have no control over. But we can always control being truthful.
OTIS

When I'm sad I make out with nerdy boys.
RUBY

When we're having sex, I feel like I've never seen a vagina before. But I have seen one, because I've got one, and I've looked at it a lot.
TANYA

You shouldn't compare the size of your genitals to anyone else's. It's irrelevant and unhelpful.
OTIS

Dreams aren't real. That's why they're called dreams.
ADAM

To be clear, I don't want to have sex with you specifically. Just a human man with a penis.
LILY

He's spoken to me exactly 26 times, using a total of 556 words.
VIV

27

2

UNDERSTANDING IDENTITY

If you've ever asked yourself the question "Who *am* I?" you're not alone. People are constantly discovering what they like, what they don't and how they feel most comfortable. Humans are ever-changing, and there can be amazing freedom in that.

But understanding and accepting yourself can also be a source of great emotional distress.

UNDERSTANDING AND **ACCEPTING YOURSELF**

Understanding your identity, who you are and who you want to be is an incredible thing. But discovering this, and then accepting it, isn't always easy. It's natural to want to fit in and not to stand out from the crowd but hiding who you truly are can be hard and have a negative effect on your mental health (see chapter ten for more info on this).

You might feel pressure from those around you, and even society in general, to think in a certain way, be attracted to one type of person or outwardly present in a way that blends in. (Why blend in when you can be fabulous, right Eric?)

> Sexuality is fluid. Sex doesn't make us whole. And so, how could you ever be broken?
> **JEAN**

28

You might feel like you can't be yourself, but confiding in those closest to you, finding a like-minded community in person or online or speaking to a professional can really help to build your confidence and make you feel less alone.

Why not try keeping a diary? Recording your thoughts and feelings can lead to better self-awareness and help you to understand and learn about yourself.

How you want to express your identity or who you are attracted to may be consistent throughout your life or it could change over time. You may even find yourself not attracted to anyone. Whatever you feel, finding a strong support system will help in the quest for self-discovery.

It might not always be easy but remember how you choose to define yourself is your decision and your identity has value.

SEXUALITY IS A
BROAD SPECTRUM

Sexual orientation (or sexual identity) is rooted in the feelings of sexual attraction you have towards other people. In the past there was no real understanding or acceptance of anything other than heterosexuality. While there are still many places where this is the case, understanding of sexuality as a more complex and nuanced issue is growing. The idea of sexuality being a spectrum allows people to think of their sexual identity in a more fluid way, rather than having to make a choice between one label or another. Many people may feel their sexual orientation is across a range, rather than a fixed point on the spectrum.

Below is a brief description of some sexual identities and it is in no way exhaustive. There are many other identities and you need to find what feels right for you, even if that means no label.

HETEROSEXUAL

Also referred to as straight, it means someone who is attracted to people of the opposite gender.

GAY OR LESBIAN

Someone who is attracted to people of the same gender.

BISEXUAL

Someone who is attracted to people of their own gender and genders different to their own.

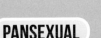

PANSEXUAL

Someone who is emotionally and/or physically attracted to all genders. Some people prefer the term pansexual to bisexual. It is sometimes described as being attracted to the person, regardless of their biological sex or gender identity.

ASEXUAL

An asexual person has little or no sexual attraction towards others, though this doesn't necessarily mean they don't engage in sexual activity.

GENDER **IDENTITY**

Although the terms sex and gender are often used interchangeably, they are not the same. A person's biological sex is assigned based on the genitals they are born with. This is generally

male and **female**

Gender relates to society's perceptions of behaviors and appearances, as well as a person's internal perception of their own identity. Some people identify with the gender they were assigned at birth while others identify differently.

As society continues to evolve, a deeper understanding of the different terms and identities is being developed.

It is up to each individual to determine how they self-identify and express their gender, and it is important that everyone's identity is respected. If you ever find yourself in a situation where someone is wilfully ignoring your identity, it can be very distressing. If you feel able, bring it up with friends or speak to a person in a position of authority to help deal with the situation. And if you are witness to an incident, it's also important to say something and back up the person if they need it. The responsibility for change and understanding shouldn't always fall on the shoulders of the marginalized.

Hope's outdated and discriminatory attitude during our sex ed class is exactly the sort of thing that those of us who identify in different ways face all the time. Even though she knew that Layla and I identify as non-binary, she went out of her way to single us out and tried to embarrass us into choosing the girls' queue. Layla felt a pressure to comply, but I wouldn't take it. How I identify is just as valid as anyone else.

CAL

Everyone has a responsibility to be understanding and to learn about and accept people's differences. It's natural to have questions about topics or issues you haven't been exposed to before, but should you ask them of someone? Some people may be more than happy to chat to a total stranger about their identity, but you should never assume, and if someone isn't comfortable speaking about the topic, respect their decision. It's important not to put the responsibility onto the person but to do the work yourself. There are plenty of helpful resources online (see the back of the book for some trusted sources). As well as gender identity, the same goes for sexuality, race and disability.

A simple thing that everyone can do is to introduce yourself with your pronoun(s) when meeting someone new. This can be especially helpful in a group situation as it can encourage everyone to do the same so no one feels the pressure of bringing the topic up.

If you have questions, or there's someone in your life who may not have much knowledge about gender identity, a simple guide to some terms is below.

Cisgender

A person who identifies with the sex they were assigned at birth.

Transgender

Transgender is often used as a sweeping term to describe gender diverse people as a whole. Transgender people identify as a different gender than the sex they were assigned at birth.

Non-binary

An umbrella term for someone who does not identify solely as being male or female. It is also sometimes used by people who reject the idea of a male and female binary altogether.

Genderqueer or gender non-conforming

If someone doesn't identify fully as either male or female, or is between or beyond genders, they may identify as genderqueer. This identity is often in reaction to gender stereotypes and the social construction of gender.

Gender fluid

A person who is gender fluid may fluctuate between genders, express themselves through multiple genders at the same time, or their gender may vary depending on circumstance.

Gender neutral

A gender-neutral person is someone who feels they are neither male or female.

Gender expression

Gender expression is about how someone expresses themselves to the world rather than about their gender or sex. A trans woman may not dress in a typically feminine way, or a cis male may wear make-up. It's about a person's behaviors and choices, and how they like to express themselves.

COMING **OUT**

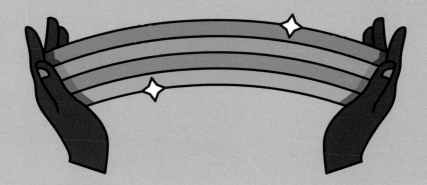

Coming out refers to a process of self-acceptance and can be a lifelong process.

Coming to terms with your sexuality or identity can be a really hard thing. Sadly, not all areas, schools or workplaces are open-minded. You may be living in a small village where you're the only non-heterosexual person you know of, and that can be exceptionally tough.

As part of your journey, you may decide you want to come out publicly. There is no right or wrong way to come out and it's totally your choice whether you tell anyone. It's your decision and you should only ever tell people when and if it feels right and safe for you.

You may feel like you want to confide in a couple of close friends and that's enough, or you may already be expressing your queerness loudly and proudly like Eric. Much like finding those elusive, perfect-fitting jeans, it is not one size fits all.

If you decide to tell your parents, depending how open-minded they are or aren't, it can be scary. If you want to let them know but you can't face doing it yourself, you could ask a sibling or another family member to talk to them on your behalf, or alongside you, if that would feel more comfortable. You could even write down what you're going to say so you're prepared, or write them a letter.

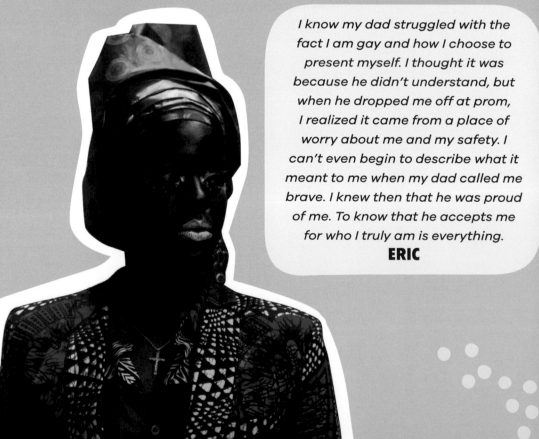

I know my dad struggled with the fact I am gay and how I choose to present myself. I thought it was because he didn't understand, but when he dropped me off at prom, I realized it came from a place of worry about me and my safety. I can't even begin to describe what it meant to me when my dad called me brave. I knew then that he was proud of me. To know that he accepts me for who I truly am is everything.

ERIC

If your friends and family struggle to accept you for who you are, it can be devastating. Sometimes the difficulty comes from a lack of understanding or worry and there are some helpful resources at the back of the book you can point people to. If you can, reach out to friends, to other family or online communities, or there are charities that offer support. Just remember you are not alone – there are always people who will be there for you.

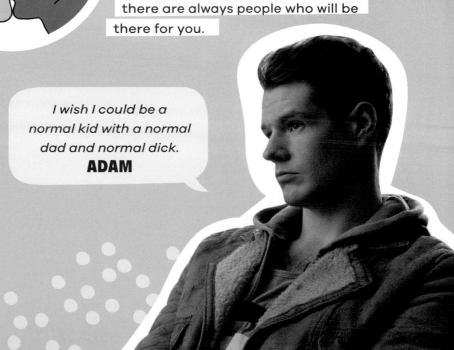

I wish I could be a normal kid with a normal dad and normal dick.
ADAM

ARE WE ALL
A LITTLE BIT ADAM?

Have you ever felt like people don't get you? Misunderstood or left out? Or maybe there's someone you think is a bit of a weirdo and don't give them the time of day? If you've answered **yes** to any of these questions, think to yourself: Adam Groff. "Adam?" you ask. "What's he got to do with it?"

Adam has to be one of the most misunderstood students at Moordale. Everyone has probably felt like nobody understands them at one time or another, but Adam, well, he doesn't just take the cake, he's the entire snack aisle of the supermarket. To the outside world Adam was a bully, he didn't care about school and was happiest when he was making other people unhappy. But underneath all that, Adam was struggling with deep unhappiness and self-doubt, in part thanks to his overly critical father, the one and only Mr. Groff.

Dealing with bullying at home is never going to be easy and Adam took out his anger on others. If you find yourself in a similar situation, know that it is not OK and you are not alone. If you feel able, try to speak to someone about what's going on at home – it could be a friend, a teacher or a relative, or consider speaking to a counselor. There are organizations you can speak to for free and confidential advice.

It's easy to lash out when you feel out of your depth or frustrated because you're under a lot of pressure or someone doesn't "get you." When the world feels too harsh, it's easy to retreat back into your shell like a little hermit crab, but that can alienate you from those around you. Once Adam had the support of friends who liked him for who he really was, he could finally be himself, stand up to his dad and, most importantly, be happy.

ADAM
Groff

JEAN'S NOTEBOOK: **SEX MYTHS**

I've been looking into some of the most common sex myths and it just shows how woeful sex education can be. It's not just teens who believe these things either; plenty of adults are still lacking in some basic knowledge. We really must do better.

Myth One
Vaginas are "tight" or "loose" depending how much sex you have had.

Completely untrue! The vagina itself is a muscle, and like other muscles in our body, it can expand and contract. When aroused, the muscles soften and lengthen to make insertion easier. If not sufficiently aroused, the muscles are contracted so insertion will be more difficult and uncomfortable.

Myth Two
You can't get pregnant if:
* It's your first time
* You pull out
* You have your period
* You are in certain positions
* You rinse with water after sex

Pregnancy occurs when sperm reaches and fertilizes an egg. Any of these examples could still result in pregnancy. Ejaculate and pre-ejaculate carry millions of sperm and you only need one to complete its journey. If you are at risk of pregnancy, think contraception.

Myth Three
You can get an STI or STD from a toilet seat.

Most STIs and STDs are transmitted through bodily fluids. This includes vaginal and anal fluids, pre-ejaculate, semen and blood. You can't catch anything from simply sitting on a toilet seat. But for any form of sexual contact, use protection.

Myth Four
Sex is only good if you have an orgasm.

The aim of sex should be pleasure for everyone involved, whether you orgasm or not. Some people find it difficult to reach orgasm, or may never experience one, but that doesn't mean sex is off the cards. Don't pressure yourself worrying about an orgasm and enjoy the experience.

Myth Five
Older people never have sex.

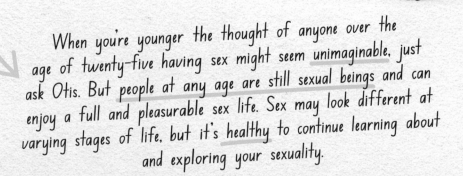

When you're younger the thought of anyone over the age of twenty-five having sex might seem unimaginable, just ask Otis. But people at any age are still sexual beings and can enjoy a full and pleasurable sex life. Sex may look different at varying stages of life, but it's healthy to continue learning about and exploring your sexuality.

3

ALL BODIES GREAT AND SMALL

Everyone has bodies, right? It's nothing to be ashamed of.
OTIS

IS MY BODY **NORMAL?**

Is there any such thing as "normal" when it comes to our bodies? **In a word, no.** Using the word normal implies that some things are abnormal and that isn't the case. Every body is different and we come in all shapes and sizes. There are big and small boobs, long and short penises, slim people, plus-sized people, bodies with medical needs and a whole lot more.

There is no such thing as a "standard" body. Some people have extra bits (Harry Styles has extra nipples) or missing bits (some people never grow pubic hair, or may have been born without certain body parts). Whether it's stretch marks, scars, burns, very large breasts or low-hanging testicles, we are all fabulously unique, just as we should be.

The availability of plastic surgery, like Brazilian butt lifts and belly button remodeling, along with social media has made comparing yourself to others even easier. If an alien landed tomorrow, found a cell phone and was drawn to a social media app, they might scroll through a hundred accounts and think that all earth women have big butts, giant boobs and lips, tiny waists and perfectly smooth skin. But you'd be hard-pushed to find a woman who looks like that checking out the discounted items at your local supermarket .

Our bodies can't magically change according to trends. It's not easy, but you need to try to learn to love your body and everything it does for you.

43

EVERYONE FEELS **INSECURE**

You might feel like you're the only one but just
know that everyone has insecurities. Maybe
your worries affect your day-to-day life or
are more occasional but they all are valid
if they affect how you feel about yourself.

Although it's much easier said than
done, the old cliché that beauty comes
from within really is true. If you can get
to a place where you feel happy in your
own body, you're winning.

But if you ever feel like how you look is
affecting your mental health, it's always better
to speak to someone about it. Confide in a close friend, speak to
a professional, flick to chapter ten for more information or take a
look at the resources listed at the back of the book.

PERFECTION IS **A BIG OLD MYTH**

We are often made to feel "less than" thanks to glossy magazines
and airbrushed social media offerings showcasing how we
should look. Even supermodels have hang-ups and compare
themselves to other models, wondering why they didn't get that
contract. They've all sobbed into a tub of dairy-free, low-fat ice
cream like everyone else.

If you know someone who has a perfect body then
congratulations – you may know the only one in the entire world.
And do you know what? It's very unlikely they think their body is
perfect and they may really envy your cute freckles (that you
might hate!) or your impressively long fingers.

44

The fashion industry is slowly moving towards using models of all shapes, sizes and ethnicities, and the body positivity movement is constantly gaining momentum. It's showing us that success isn't about looking a certain way; it's about embracing who you are, from dressing in a way that makes you smile no matter your size, to the scars that tell a story or how you rock a colorful scarf. And please don't think for a minute that people are sitting around for hours analyzing you either. Everyone is way too busy thinking about their own hang-ups to give yours more than half a second's thought.

Even if you do cross someone's mind, you may well be one of many people they're having critical thoughts about that day.

Unhappy people love to find flaws in other people for one reason – because they're down on themselves and it makes them feel better.
MAEVE

People who are happy in their own skin (even those with a long list of so-called "imperfections") don't need to put others down to feel good. Who would you rather be?

Your skin suit and all its internal workings does its best for you, even if it needs a little help from time to time. It will always fight as hard as it can to keep you healthy. So give your body a hug, some gratitude and a big old high five.

YOUR BODY IS BIZARRE BUT BRILLIANT

Some totally random things you probably didn't know about your body (and possibly don't need to know, but think how cool you'll look if they pop up in a quiz):

✳ The human body contains around eight pints of blood.

✳ If you laid out all the blood vessels in your body, they could circle the world four times.

✳ More than half of your bones are located in the hands and feet.

✳ Your heart beats approximately 100,000 times a day.

✳ The human nose can detect around one trillion smells (why does BO have to be one of them?).

✳ Thumbs have their own pulse.

✳ If you blush, your stomach lining turns red (in solidarity?).

WHAT'S *THAT* **BIT FOR?**

OK, it's time to get into it. Here's all you need to know about everything down there, and what does what.

THE VAGINA

It's where fingers, sex toys, tampons, menstrual cups, contraception devices and penises go in. If you aren't practicing safe sex, it's also where babies can come out.

> *Why celebrate the day I got pushed out of some random vagina against my will?*
> **MAEVE**

People often use the word vagina as a general term for the whole package, but it actually refers to the birth canal, which leads to your uterus. So it's a bit like a cul-de-sac in that it's an enclosed area; anything that goes into the vagina has no chance of working its way up into the rest of your body (always a relief). The vulva describes the external genitalia that surround the opening to the vagina.

LET'S GET TECHNICAL

If you are born with female reproductive parts, eggs and the hormones estrogen and progesterone are formed in the ovaries. The ovaries are connected to the fallopian tubes and are where eggs travel to reach the uterus during ovulation.

The uterus is in the lower abdomen and is where a baby grows. As part of the menstrual cycle, roughly every 28 days, the lining of the uterus thickens in preparation for an egg being fertilized by sperm. If this doesn't happen, the lining is shed, resulting in a period. Periods usually begin around age twelve, but it can be earlier or later. Most periods last between three and eight days, with bleeding usually heaviest the first two. On your heaviest days, the blood will be red, while lighter days it might be pink, brown or black.

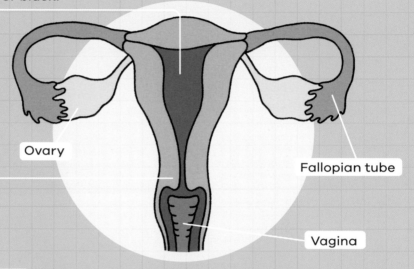

Ovary

Fallopian tube

Vagina

The cervix is a part of your uterus that extends into your vagina. It's also the part doctors collect cells from when you go for a pap smear. Most of the time the cervix door is shut, but it opens to release blood and mucus when periods come a-knocking, and it also dilates before someone gives birth.

Endometriosis is a condition where tissue similar to the lining of the womb grows in the ovaries or fallopian tubes and it can be extremely painful. It's not clear what causes endometriosis but some symptoms are very bad pain during your period, pain during or after sex, feeling sick, feeling constipated or having diarrhea during your period. If you experience any unusual symptoms during your period, it is always best to speak to a doctor to get it checked out.

Confused about how a vagina can fit a baby through it but can also keep hold of a tampon or menstrual cup for hours? Here's why. When a vagina is relaxed, the pressure of the surrounding organs and tissues cause the vaginal walls to collapse against each other and allow tampons to stay in place.

The walls of the vagina release fluids to help keep the vagina clean, moist and protected from infection. It's also responsible for increasing lubrication when sexually aroused. Vaginal discharge is nothing to worry about unless you notice a change in its smell, color or texture, then It's best to visit a doctor to have it checked out.

The labia majora, also known as the outer lips (labia is Latin for lips), form part of the vulva and protect the more sensitive internal parts of the vajayjay. They are the ones that are covered in pubic hair.

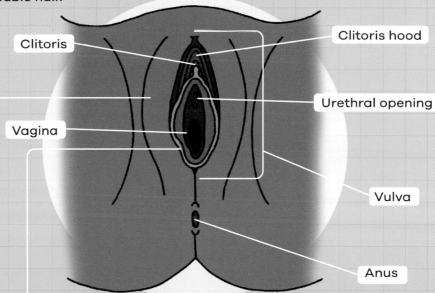

- Clitoris
- Clitoris hood
- Urethral opening
- Vagina
- Vulva
- Anus

The labia minora, or inner lips, are like the second line of defense for what lies within. They have magic (well, not strictly *magic*) oil glands that lubricate your vagina to keep it feeling comfortable.

There is no one size fits all when it comes to labia majora or minora. They come in all shapes and sizes, aren't always symmetrical and almost certainly don't look like those of porn stars. See chapter eight for more on this.

The small hole you pee out of, the urethral opening, is positioned right below the clitoris. If you used to think you peed out of your vagina, you're not alone.

The hymen is a thin piece of skin inside the opening of the vagina. It doesn't cover the full vaginal opening, which is how menstrual blood is able to flow through. It's also common to be born without a hymen.

Contrary to popular belief, the hymen doesn't "break" when a person first has sex because it is already perforated, but it may stretch or tear, which can cause bleeding. In some cases, the hymen may already have been stretched due to the use of tampons, playing sports or masturbation. That means it is impossible to tell whether someone has had sex or not simply by looking at their hymen.

SMALL BUT MIGHTY

It's an often overlooked part of the anatomy, but when it comes to the **clitoris**, less is definitely more. The clitoris contains 8,000 nerve endings, making it the go-to if someone wants to achieve an orgasm on their own or with another person, so it's important to know where it is and what to do with it.

The clitoral hood is a small flap of skin that covers the clitoris to ward off any unwanted irritation or arousal in everyday life (and help avoid embarrassing scenes in the supermarket line). When you are aroused, the hood slides back so your clitoris is free to drink in all the pleasure it can handle.

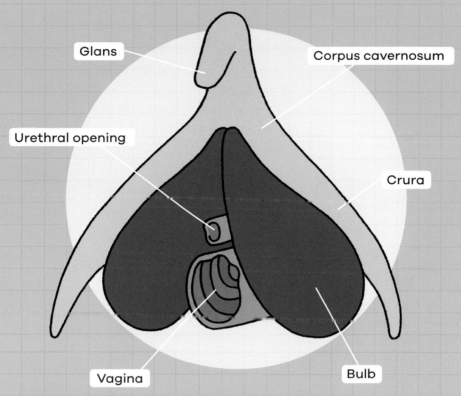

Glans

Corpus cavernosum

Urethral opening

Crura

Vagina

Bulb

Did you know the clitoris is mainly internal? A relatively recent anatomical discovery, the inside structure of the clitoris extends from the external love button and splits in half like two lovely legs (known as the crura) with two vestibular bulbs (elongated masses of erectile tissue) between the crura and the vagina.

The legs make their way down through, and behind, the labia minora, past the urethra and vaginal canal, and extend towards the anus. When you are in the throes of passion, the crura and vestibular bulbs swell on either side of the vagina increasing lubrication, sexual stimulation and sensation.

Sound the bloody horns!

THE **PENIS**

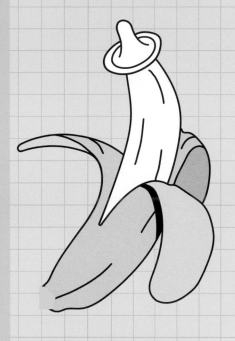

Research suggests that the average penis is between thirteen to eighteen centimetres (or five to seven inches) when erect. You cannot make it bigger using exercises, medication or using tablets bought from the internet. Any tablets advertized online (often on porn sites) will not make your penis larger, and as they are unregulated, they could potentially be dangerous.

PENIS FACTS

The penis is made up of two chambers called corpora cavernosum (anyone else think that sounds like a fancy pizza?) that run the entire length of the penis, and are made up of a maze of sponge-like blood vessels.

The urethra, a tube through which semen and urine are secreted, runs along the underside of the corpora cavernosum. The urethra is surrounded by erectile tissue, with two main arteries and a selection of nerves and veins.

When the penis is erotically stimulated (i.e., when you're turned on), the corpora cavernosum relaxes, allowing blood to flow in to the spongey spaces. The blood creates pressure making the penis expand and —

ta-da- we have an erection!

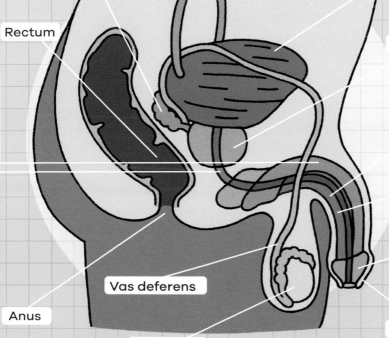

Seminal vesicle

Bladder

Rectum

Prostate gland

Corpus spongiosum

Frenulum

Vas deferens

Glans (head of the penis)

Anus

Foreskin

Testicles

The head or bell-end of the penis actually has an official name – the glans. The glans houses the urethral opening, which is the opening to the urethra.

The official name of the long part of the penis is the shaft. Nicknames include the joystick, gearshift, hot dog or meat rod. And they're the cleaner ones.

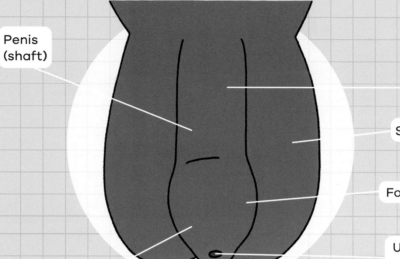

Penis (shaft)

Scrotum

Foreskin

Urethral opening

The glans is often more sensitive than the shaft. In fact, the frenulum, also referred to as the "banjo string," is found on the underside of the glans and is said to be the most sensitive part of the penis. Sometimes the frenulum can rip or bleed during vigorous sex or masturbation. If that happens, it's always best to consult a doctor to check everything is ok.

Some people have foreskins, and some don't, depending on their religious leanings or certain medical issues that call for it to be removed. Or just because they prefer to get it snipped off.

If you have a foreskin, when the penis isn't erect it covers the glans, but when it stands to attention, the foreskin automatically gets pulled back for the big reveal.

I think if I had an extra arm growing in between my legs, I might want to show everyone too.
LILY

It's very common for younger men to have tight foreskins, which can become a source of worry, especially as most men shown in porn have either been circumcised or have easily retractable foreskins. However, unless it causes soreness, swelling or redness, which could be an indication of a condition called phimosis, there is no need to consult a doctor.

The testicles live in the scrotum (the wrinkly sack-like numbers) and are also super sensitive.

If you've always thought that semen and sperm were the same thing, prepare to have your mind blown.

Semen, also known as cum or ejaculate, is what shoots out of the penis when you come, while sperm are male reproductive cells and are just one component of semen. Semen itself is made up of mature sperm, fluids from the prostate, bulbourethral glands and seminal vesicles, mucus, sugars, protein and vitamins.

The perineum, the area between the anus and the penis, is very sensitive, and can be used to stimulate the prostate, a part of the reproductive system where the seminal fluid is made. Think of it as a walnut-sized semen factory.

SIDE NOTE: the prostrate can be prone to problems and become inflamed. In the best-case scenario it's caused by a relatively harmless condition called prostatitis, and worse case it can be prostate cancer. If you ever notice any changes in that area, always get it checked by your doctor. It's incredibly common to get swelling and it's definitely nothing to be embarrassed about.

Seminal fluid mixes with sperm from the testes to help the sperm stay safe and travel well (like a sexual travel agent). Semen's job is basically to protect the little tadpole-shaped sperm so they're ready to swim off and fertilize an egg. Without semen to carry them, sperm would keep swimming around in circles like goldfish in a bowl.

On average, 200 million sperm are released during each ejaculation and it takes just one – one! – to fertilize an egg. Semen shoots out of the urethra like a bullet out of a gun, and usually takes the form of a sticky, clear or whitish liquid, although color and consistency can vary. If it's yellow or green and it smells, the chances are there's some infection and it needs looking at ASAP.

Contrary to popular belief, you cannot break a penis, because it isn't made of bone. You can, however, damage it if you manhandle it too roughly.

Ejaculating is healthy and it's recommended to do it several times a week, so fill your boots.

You jizzed your pants, you're not Hannibal Lector.
ERIC

INTERSEX

Not everyone has sexual anatomy that can be classified as male or female. Intersex is a term that is used to cover people who are born with, or develop, differences in their sex traits or reproductive anatomy. There is no one characteristic that defines intersex; there are many differences that can occur in genitalia, internal anatomy or hormones. It's estimated that around 1.7 percent of people born are intersex while others may not develop traits until puberty or later in life. It isn't possible to "spot" an intersex person; they are as diverse as the rest of the world.

Many intersex people are subjected to surgery when they are very young as there is still a lot of shame and stigma associated with not conforming to the binary. Because of this stigma, some intersex folks might struggle with shame or uncertainty about their bodies. But no one should be forced into having any medical procedures they can't consent to themselves.

If you feel that you may be intersex, there are great communities online and around the world that offer support and friendship. See some resources at the back of the book.

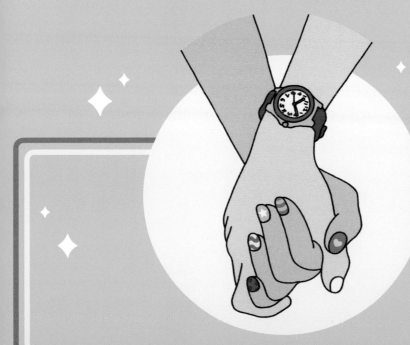

HAVE YOU HAD **YOUR HAIR DONE?**

There is a huge amount of pressure on women to remove their pubic hair these days, but it's totally your choice. Pubic hair is natural, most people grow it when they hit puberty – the amount and color depends on the person. If you don't want to remove any or all of your pubic hair, that's completely fine. Many people love to embrace their natural look – and just think of how much time and money you'll save.

If, however, you are tempted to try pubic hair grooming, there are a multitude of options:

I love my full bush! **OLA**

triangle
(a little bit at the top, so your labia majora is hair-free)

bikini line
(a neater version of the full bush)

landing strip
(similar to the triangle but hair is shaped in a thin line)

a Brazilian
(completely bare)

Those who are feeling adventurous might even like to try:

the moustache

the lightning bolt

the heart

the arrow

When it comes to those of you with a penis, it's becoming more popular to shave, cut or shape pubic hair to make a willy look bigger, better or more coiffured. Is it acceptable? Of course, but be mindful that undercuts are a step too far.

Whether you're shaving, using hair removal cream or waxing (which should ideally be done professionally!), remember that the skin in that area is pretty sensitive, so factor in a little bit of recovery time.

RECOVERY TIME

ADVICE FROM
MOORDALE'S SEXPERTS

When Otis and Maeve set up the sex clinic, they could probably never have imagined some of the problems they'd be dealing with. Were they always right? Ummmm . . . no. But they do have some good advice:

You can't __CHOOSE__ who you're attracted to. You can't. You can't engineer a relationship.

Sometimes the people we like don't like us back. It's painful, but there's __NOTHING__ we can do about it.

You should work with what you've got.

We all mess up and do impure things. It doesn't mean we're bad people.

You need to own your narrative. Not let it control you.

You have to __ACCEPT__ the imperfect parts of people, too.

Fairy tales are all about female suppression.

LOVE AND RELATIONSHIPS

Love isn't about grand gestures, or the moon and the stars. It's just dumb luck. And sometimes, you meet someone who feels the same way. And then sometimes you're unlucky. But one day, you're going to meet someone who appreciates you for who you are. I mean, there are seven billion people on the planet. I know one of them is going to climb up on a moon for you.

OTIS MILBURN

LOVE GURU AND TEENAGE PHILOSOPHER

YOUR CRUSH IS COMING, **ACT NORMAL**

So there's someone out there that you just can't stop thinking about. Maybe you feel a rush of excitement when you see them, or get butterflies in your stomach every time you think about them. No matter what you do you can't help feeling the feels – you've got a crush.

You can't control who you get a crush on, it's just one of life's great mysteries, like why peanut butter and jelly tastes so good or that a passport photo will always be terrible. Your crush could be a Hollywood superstar or someone you've seen around town – a lot of crushes are a fun, healthy way to discover what you want both from a partner and a relationship. But a crush can also be confusing and a cause of real worry and anxiety.

Maybe you've gone your whole life not thinking about your sexuality and then find you can't stop thinking about someone who is the same gender as you. Does this mean you're gay? Bisexual? (Refer back to chapter two for more on understanding identity.) Having strong feelings for someone of the same gender can be part of growing up. As you learn more about who you are, you may decide you want to identify in a certain way or you might prefer not to label yourself.

There is no right or wrong when it comes to your feelings, but at times it may feel overwhelming. If you feel able to, it can help to speak to a trusted friend, a professional or clinics for help and advice. Some great places are listed at the back of this book.

When I first started at Moordale, Lily and I were just friends. She was really there for me through everything with Otis and I found myself thinking about her more and more. I'd never had feelings for another girl before and, to be honest, I found it quite confusing. But then I realized that I don't need to be limited by old-fashioned thinking around sexuality – I was attracted to Lily as a person, it didn't matter if she was male or female. Realizing that I was pansexual and taking ownership of my identity is something to be proud of.

OLA

What if the person you like is really into cosplay? Surely if you line your wardrobes with a variety of character outfits they'll like you back, right? Well, not necessarily. You shouldn't feel you need to look or act a certain way to get someone to like you. It's easy to get caught up in your feelings and want to impress someone or feel like you have a connection. But a true connection can only come if you're being yourself. And if your thing is actually K-Pop, you're much more likely to meet someone you really click with at that K-Pop convention you've been dying to go to.

Most of the time, crushes disappear as quickly as they arrive. One day you're lusting over the star of your favorite TV show, then suddenly you find yourself imagining a long, happy life with the hot stranger you saw on the bus.

Crushes don't always have to be romantic, either. Sometimes we can have friendship crushes, where we feel really close to someone and really admire them. Or we like the way someone dresses, or their attitude, or how they make us feel when we're around them.

We can also have virtual crushes, where we never ever meet a friend in person, but we feel super close to them via online chats or WhatsApp messages, connecting through social media or video calls. This is perfectly normal and healthy, and lockdowns have made these ways of connecting and bonding with people even more popular.

Occasionally, though, a crush can become an infatuation. If you find yourself thinking about someone so much you can't concentrate or make excuses not to see your friends so you can daydream about them, it could be time to revaluate and talk to someone about your feelings.

OH, WHAT A SURPRISE TO SEE **YOU HERE!**

You really like someone and you've decided you need to know if they like you, too – so what now? Well, first things first, you need to speak to them.

If you can do this face-to-face, that's great. Chatting to someone in real life is always a good option – the tried and true "accidental meeting" can be an easy way to strike up a casual conversation. If you don't feel comfortable introducing yourself, you can ask a friend to put you in contact if you've got mutual acquaintances. Perhaps you feel shy or awkward in person and might feel more confident chatting to someone via your phone so could try connecting with them over social media. This can give you time to think about your responses without some of the anxiety. But if you're going to contact someone online, please make sure you are sure you know who they are first – read chapter eight for more info on keeping safe online.

Once you've been speaking for a while and if you're feeling brave, you can always suggest a meet up. If you don't ask, you don't get and someone's got to make the first move.

> *You have to let the people you love know that you love them, even if it causes you a great deal of pain.*
> **MAUREEN**

LOVE ME, **LOVE ME NOT**

One of life's hardest lessons is that everyone will have to deal with rejection at some point. Trying for something that you want and not being accepted, whether that be making new friends, jobs or potential relationships, is always difficult to deal with.

If you really like someone and muster up the courage to ask them out, it can be devastating when they say no. It's common for rejection to make you feel insecure or like you're not good enough, but it's something that happens to everyone – even Beyoncé has to deal with rejection sometimes. The most important thing to try and remember is that there is nothing wrong with you, and that there is nothing wrong with the person who has rejected you, either. Everyone is entitled to their own opinion and feelings and, hard as it may be, you just need to feel the heartbreak, accept the emotions and try to move on.

TO KISS OR **NOT TO KISS?**

The path of romance is littered with minefields and here's another one – the first kiss. Whether it's your first, first kiss, or you've had some practice, going in for a kiss with someone new can still be nerve-wracking.

There is no right or wrong time for a first kiss, if the mood strikes and you feel they're into it too, just go with what feels right. Remember that they're probably as nervous as you are. Everyone has to have their first kiss some time and the best thing you can do is relax and try to enjoy it. And if things do go a bit awry and you accidentally headbutt each other? Try to just laugh it off – at least it gives you something to talk about.

If you're not feeling it and they go in for a kiss, don't feel pressure to reciprocate it's best to be honest about these things and just 'fess up if you don't think you like them.

WHAT'S THE DEAL **WITH DATING?**

When it comes to dating, sometimes there can be more to consider than simply where serves the best pizza in town. When choosing a good date location, you should think about where suits you and your date best. Where will you feel comfortable? Is the venue LGBTQ+ friendly? Will there be accessibility issues if you or your date have certain requirements? Would you both feel safe getting to and from the date?

If you want to be able to relax and enjoy yourself, don't feel pressure to plan the "perfect" date; it doesn't exist. Be honest, are you really going to have fun eating a six-course tasting menu based on the music of Lady Gaga, when all you both really want is a kebab and a Coke? Planning something you can *both* get on board with is the key to a good date – and what that looks like is only something you can decide.

> *When Adam and I went on a double date with Otis and Ruby it started off very awkward. I was desperate for it to just end but then weirdly Ruby and Adam starting bonding over the Kardashians of all people! Some people really do surprise you.*
> **ERIC**

LOCK IT **DOWN**

Once you've been dating someone for a while it can feel like you're floating on air. But it can also often be fraught with a worry that things may not work out and you want to know when you can relax. But when will that be? When?

Every relationship is different, the only thing that will help is time. Either you'll come to realize that this relationship isn't the one for you, or one day you're no longer worrying about whether they like you as much as you like them.

Just be aware that one of you might want to make things official more quickly than the other and that's OK. You may not both be on the same page at exactly the same time but that doesn't have to mean disaster. No one knows what's coming because we are human beings with human feelings that can change constantly, so take things day by day and try to enjoy them. The trick is not to rush things or put pressure on the other person to commit.

If your mind starts propelling you into the realms of marriage and kids within weeks of meeting someone, remember to consider how the other person feels. It's fine to daydream about your life together, living by the sea with a couple of weiner dogs, but it's probably best to keep it to yourself for now.

> *Commitment can be a frightening prospect.*
> **JEAN**

THE **"L" WORD**

Love – a topic the world's greatest thinkers have been mulling over for years. There are countless books, films and songs dedicated to the feeling, but what is love?

Love is not easily defined and it doesn't need to refer to romantic love. There's the love you might feel for your family, your friends, your pets, your favorite musician, a specific person. And even though they're all different, they're also somehow the same. It's a feeling you get, and sometimes don't even realize it's there.

Love means different things to different people, and whenever and however you feel it, is what love means to you.

> *I don't think any of us really understand much about love except that when we feel it, we feel it.*
> **JEAN**

When it comes to saying "I love you," there isn't a right or wrong way or time. All relationships are unique, and while some couples may say those three little words within days of dating, others take months, or may never reach that stage at all.

Some people turn saying "I love you" into a grand gesture with flowers and chocolates, while others blurt it out without thinking. Just remember, once it's out there, you can't take it back.

It's always a risk because someone has to say it first, but you should commend yourself for your bravery. If someone doesn't say it back, it doesn't necessarily mean they're never going to; it could just be that your feelings have intensified quicker than theirs. But you also need to be prepared for the fact they may not feel the same.

> *When Ruby said she loved me it came as a shock, maybe that was obvious by my reply, "That's nice." I still cringe thinking about it. But I just couldn't say it back to her. I didn't feel the same way and it would have been unfair to both of us if I had. I know I should have thought of a better response but it was the only thing that came to me in the moment. I'm not always great when I'm put on the spot but isn't it situations like this that make us all human? What's more important is that I spoke to her about it afterwards; honesty is the best policy.*
> **OTIS**

If you don't feel the feels, it's unfair to pretend you do just to make things less awkward. You should only say I love you when you really feel it, whether that fits into someone else's idea of your relationship's timeline or not.

> *You know in rom-coms, when the guy finally realizes he's in love with the girl and he turns up with a boom box outside her house, blasting her favorite song and everyone in the audience swoons? Yeah, that makes me sick.*
> **MAEVE**

BREAKUPS **(ARE CRAP)**

There's no getting away from it – everyone will probably have their heart broken at least once in their life. And when it happens, it really sucks. Breakups and rejection bring with them a special kind of pain that feels like no other. It sticks a giant needle into the most fragile parts of you and can make you question everything about yourself, dragging your self-esteem into the gutter in the process. The *what's wrong with mes* can circle around your head like a shark hunting for its dinner.

Sadly there are no quick cures for heartache. Talking to someone close to you, writing about how you feel, having a good cry – it all can really help. The worst thing you can do is bottle up your emotions. Painful as it might be, it's always better to deal with them. The only true healer is time – what one day feels unbearable will slowly fade and eventually you'll feel like yourself again.

If you're in a relationship with someone who really likes you and you're not feeling it any more, it's not cool to hang around because it's the easy option. No matter how hard the breakup might be, you have to be truthful and let them know.

There might be times in your life when you meet someone you like and you both agree you're happy with a loose arrangement that isn't leading to anything serious. As long as you're both on the same page, and one of you isn't secretly hoping for more, then there's nothing wrong with having fun. At least then you've always got back-up for those impossible to get out of family get-togethers.

We've been holding hands for 45 minutes. I know how to hold hands. I'm here to fornicate.
LILY

By staying in a relationship you're no longer happy in, you're also doing yourself a disservice. There's no reason you can't do all the things you want to do flying solo (have a look at chapter eleven for some tips on happiness). You're also stopping yourself from potentially meeting someone who really gets you. **So don't delay, dump today** (in absolutely the kindest way possible).

Ghosting them ✖

Sending them a message ✖

Blocking them on social media ✖

Posting a photo of you with someone else and hope they get the message ✖

Getting a friend to tell them ✖

Speaking to them face to face ✔

If you're doing the breaking up, try to speak to them in person or, if you're long distance, over a video call. Explain your reasons clearly – write them down if you have to – and give them a chance to ask questions so they don't leave the conversation with a head full of whys. It may be more painful in the short term but, by being totally upfront, they will hopefully heal more quickly.

If you know you're going to see them around, discuss how you're going to handle it so you don't have to worry about that hideously awkward first-time run-in. Don't try to stay friends with them if they're just not ready. Give them all the space they need, and maybe one day you can be friends.

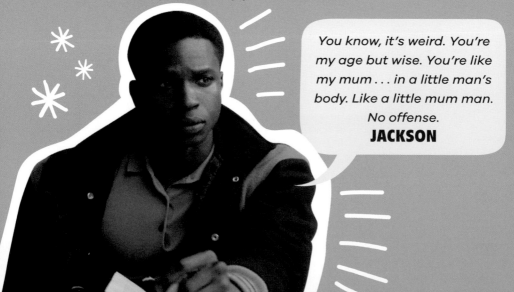

You know, it's weird. You're my age but wise. You're like my mum . . . in a little man's body. Like a little mum man. No offense.
JACKSON

If someone asks for space or to break contact, it's important to respect their boundaries. It can be tough if you still really like them, but you need to accept that the relationship is over and it is not OK to call, message or visit them in person. If a former partner is contacting you against your wishes, speak to friends or family for support. If the behavior continues or you feel at all unsafe, you can contact the police to report any post-break-up harassment or stalking.

One truly great piece of advice:
DO NOT get that breakup haircut. You will regret it.

When you love a person, there's always a tiny part of you that's terrified that one day you're going to lose them.
MAUREEN

RECOGNIZING A
BAD RELATIONSHIP

Sadly, not all relationships are about finding new ways to spell out "I love you" using emojis, and cozy nights on the couch. Sometimes things can take a dark turn and you may find yourself in an emotionally or physically abusive relationship.

Emotional abuse can be so subtle you may not even realize it's going on until it's affecting your whole life. Abusers keep chipping away day after day. It might start with the odd put-down and progress to full-on gaslighting, a behavior that leaves you questioning yourself and apologizing for things you didn't even realize you'd done wrong. The likelihood is that's because you haven't, but that's how mind games and manipulation work.

It's common for abusers to be very controlling over everything you do; before you know it, you're changing your clothes because they don't like your outfit and asking for permission to spend time with your friends. Separating you from friends and family is a common tactic of abuse – the more you rely on them, the more control they have.

Physical abuse means someone is violent towards you. Victims of abuse can start to believe that they are genuinely the one in the wrong, and that if only they were less annoying or stupid or flirty, things would be OK. But that is never the case. If you are in a situation where you are fearful of your other half, you need to get help immediately.

After a violent episode your partner may apologize, say they feel terrible and that they'll never do it again. As tempting as it is to believe, it is very rarely the truth. If someone has physically hurt you once, the chances are they will do it again.

Here's the thing; abusers often don't change — some may not even think they're being abusive, and those that do often don't know how to be any different. Whatever the underlying issue, it is not your job to help them deal with it — that's a job for a professional. Your physical and mental health are more important.

It can be very difficult to leave an abusive relationship; you may not realize how bad things are, your self-esteem may be shattered and you might even feel responsible for the other person. But any type of abuse is not OK, and there is always a way out, even if it doesn't feel like it when you're in the thick of it. If you don't have anyone in your life you can talk to, there are anonymous helplines you can call for support and advice. If you ever feel in immediate danger, always call the police.

TALKING ALWAYS HELPS

Remember that you, and your safety, are always the number-one priority.

LEARNING TO BE
HAPPY BEING SINGLE

We get it, being single can feel like the worst thing in the world when all your friends are sharing their loved-up status on social media and you're sitting at home bingeing *RuPaul's Drag Race*, hoping that the person you're secretly in love with will magically drop you a casual message.

Sadly, it usually doesn't work like that. As the magnificent RuPaul himself says, "Fulfilment isn't found over the rainbow, it's found in the here and now."

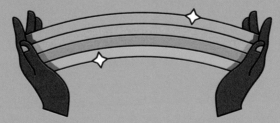

And who says being single is so bad, anyway? Plenty of people are perfectly happy being by themselves and may never want to be in a relationship. You don't need a partner to fulfil you or make you "whole" because that implies you are half a person to begin with (right or left side?).

It is always better to be alone than be with a person who doesn't make you happy, just for the sake of being with someone. If you're using up your energy trying to keep a miserable relationship going, how are you going to have the energy to be happy?

There are tons of resources online with helpful self-esteem and relationship advice because there's no doubt about it, the two go hand in hand. Check out our list of resources at the back of the book for some good sites. If you want a healthy, balanced relationship, you've got to get the most important relationship sorted out first – the one with yourself.

When Eric said to me, "It's kind of hard to like someone who doesn't like themself," it hurt. I knew he was right, but it was still difficult to hear. It's hard for me to express my feelings, I'm still figuring out who I really am and what I want. I am trying to be nicer to myself, but it's not easy. I want to be with Eric, but I need to figure out who I am on my own and learn to truly accept myself.

ADAM

The moral of this story is, you absolutely cannot rely on someone else to make you feel good about yourself. Do that, and you're going to be stuck on the misery merry-go-round forever. If you can learn to be happy and content single, you're basically winning at life.

YOU'RE NOT GETTING
IT ALL WRONG

Unfortunately, love and romance don't come with a failsafe instruction manual. If you feel anxious, insecure, scared or wary of relationships, welcome to the world of dating. Just know that everyone has been there, even the ones who seem to have it all figured out. In love, just like in life, everyone is simply doing the best they can and learning along the way.

At times it might be difficult or painful or confusing but as cliché as it may sound, we can all only learn and grow by trying our best and living each day as it comes.

IT'S ALL ABOUT **RESPECT**

When it comes to behavior towards women or anyone female-presenting, as Aretha Franklin says,

RESPECT.

Respect isn't just for relationships. Everyone is responsible for their own behavior towards others and it's up to you as an individual to ensure the way you act is appropriate and respectful. Shouting out in the street, making inappropriate comments, intimidating behavior or attempting to embarrass or humiliate people is always unacceptable. Saying,

IT'S JUST A JOKE!

isn't an excuse.

There can be a lot of pressure to act a certain way to fit in with the "guys" but that kind of behavior hurts everyone, you included.

No one should have to alter the way they live in order to feel safe going about their day-to-day life. **THAT'S ON YOU, FELLAS.**

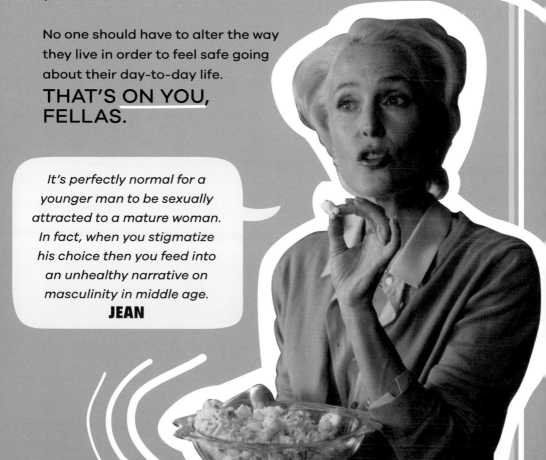

It's perfectly normal for a younger man to be sexually attracted to a mature woman. In fact, when you stigmatize his choice then you feed into an unhealthy narrative on masculinity in middle age.
JEAN

I USE A WHEELCHAIR.
SO WHAT?

People make all sorts of assumptions about me. Some days it's hurtful; others it makes me laugh. Sometimes I have a little fun with people and make up elaborate stories about why I'm in a wheelchair – you should see their faces! Here are some of the most common things people think when they first see me:

1 **I'm shy**
I think it's pretty clear, I'm not.

2 **I should be shy**
Being in a wheelchair isn't a personality trait. I'm loud, not afraid to speak my mind and like to have a laugh, just like anyone else. My disability doesn't define who I am.

3 **My life is boring**
The amazing thing about wheelchairs is that they move! I go shopping, I meet up with friends, I read a lot and I have plenty of hobbies, including painting, which I love.

4 **I can't do anything for myself**
Yes, I need help with some things, but I can do a hell of a lot for myself. Doesn't everyone need help from time to time anyway? There's no shame in asking for help when you need it. Are you telling me you do all your own washing and cleaning?

5 **I'm only friends with disabled people**
Sure, sometimes it's nice to speak to people who understand some of the difficulties I face, but being disabled isn't on my friendship application form. I'm friends with people I get on with, just like everyone else!

6 I'm required to answer any question about my disability

I know it's tempting to ask why someone's in a wheelchair, and I've lost count of the amount of people who have said, "What happened to you?" Respect boundaries, people! If you have questions, maybe try doing some research on your own, or at least ask if the person is happy to discuss their disability. If they say no, don't ask anyway! Nobody should have to answer personal questions if they don't want to – would you like it if I asked your medical history?

7 I don't think about sex

Why wouldn't I?

8 I can't have sex

I can and I do. Not everyone is the same – some people might not have full function or can't get an erection. But that doesn't mean they can't want or enjoy any sexual activity and it can offer great opportunities for exploration and creativity! Remember, sex can look different for all kinds of people.

9 I only fancy other people with disabilities

That's like saying I only fancy people whose name also begins with the letter I. It makes no sense. I fancy Maeve because she's fun, cool and hot, pure and simple.

10 I should be grateful if someone fancies me

Just because I use a wheelchair doesn't mean I have to accept the first person who shows any interest. I'm handsome, I'm funny, I'm smart and I'd make a really good boyfriend. What can I say, I'm a catch!

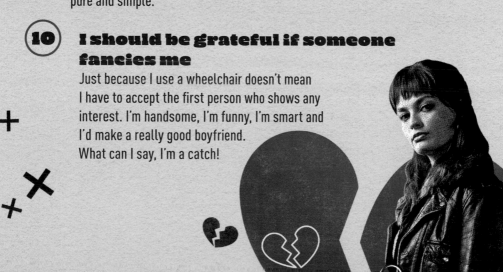

5

LOSE THE SHAME, KEEP THE PLEASURE

Whether you're already doing it, thinking about doing it, or planning to wait for a good few years, it's important to be properly clued up about s-e-x.

The most important thing to remember is that although a lot of sex education is lacking and may lead you to believe that sex is something to be talked about in hushed tones, there is nothing shameful about it. Thinking about it, talking about it, doing it – literally nothing.

Sexual pleasure has always existed, even if it isn't always acknowledged, and desiring someone, having wonderful lustful thoughts, and the sexual acts themselves are all perfectly natural parts of life. Think about it; if they weren't,

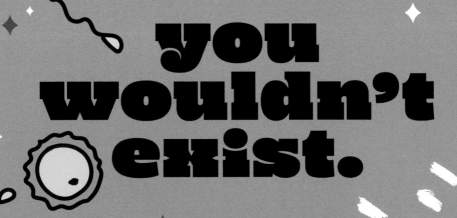

you wouldn't exist.

CAN'T TAKE MY EYES **OFF YOU**

You're with someone and you REALLY like them. You think you might be ready for the next step, but what does that mean and are you *actually* ready?

Everyone is different and will move at a different pace, but here are some important things to consider when thinking about sex and intimacy.

1 Being intimate with someone doesn't have to involve taking your clothes off. It can mean kissing, cuddling and spending time really getting to know each other.

2 Sex doesn't just mean going "all the way"; anything that makes you feel aroused is a sexual experience. There are plenty of things you can experiment with and it's not a case of having to work your way through every sexual act as quickly as you can because you feel you should. Try what you and your partner feel comfortable with, when you're both ready and you know you're going to enjoy it.

3 Every sexual experience should be intentional and desired by both people. You should never feel pressured, or pressure someone yourself, into trying something. When it comes to sex and intimacy, everything you do should be about pleasure.

4 The only "right" time to have a sexual experience is when you decide to. It's not because your partner wants to or because some of your friends have done it. FYI, people often lie about their sex lives – it's highly likely a lot of the people who brag about it haven't actually done half of those things. Take things at your own pace. The right time for you is when you've thought about it properly and you're genuinely ready – for the right reasons.

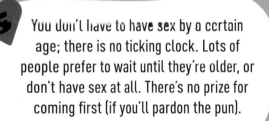

5 You don't have to have **sex** by a certain age; there is no ticking clock. Lots of people prefer to wait until they're older, or don't have sex at all. There's no prize for coming first (if you'll pardon the pun).

6 The traditional idea of virginity covers a narrow concept of sex – penetrative sex between a man and a woman. For many couples, this isn't the case so it's important to remember sex can refer to a broad spectrum of experiences.

ALL ABOUT **CONSENT**

Let's discuss consent – it's one of the most important things to know when talking about sex.

The legal age of consent in the US is eighteen, which means if you are under eighteen you are considered to be too young to give your consent to have sex. Depending where you live, the legal age of consent may vary so please find out what laws apply to you. It's always wise to be educated about the laws around sex to protect both yourself and the person you're with.

Sexual consent means that you and the person you're with want to do something sexual, whether that's kissing, touching or a sexual act, and that you are both freely making the choice. Whatever stage you are at, you should always check in with the other person to make sure they are happy and vice versa.

Consent is essential and doesn't just mean someone saying

YES or NO.

It's important to read any signs your partner is giving through:

Their body language, eye contact and facial expressions.

Are they displaying enthusiastic consent in the way they move and look at you?

Are they giving you positive signs that they are enjoying the experience and feel comfortable?

Conversely, do they seem uncomfortable?

Or are they showing physical discomfort and being quiet or nervous?

And remember no always means no and it must be respected.

IT'S MY VAGINA

Once you are in a situation it can sometimes feel difficult to vocalize your discomfort, or ask a person to stop, but it's really important to say what you are feeling. Be mindful of your partner, too – someone may say yes to something because they feel like they should, but is their demeanor giving you a big no? If you're in any doubt, the key is honest and open communication.

TALKING ALWAYS HELPS

Just because you're in a relationship with someone it doesn't mean it's an unwritten rule that you have to do what the other person wants. Far from it! And even if you have agreed to do something before, it doesn't mean you're obligated to do it again.

It's your body and nobody else has the right to it unless you give the OK. If another person does something to you against your will, that is assault and it is illegal. For more detail on sexual assault, check out chapter nine.

TOUCH ME **THERE**

Sexual desire is a completely natural part of life and something you can feel anytime, anywhere. You could wake up feeling ultra-horny and not be able to shake the feeling all day, or you may pass someone on the street that makes your legs feel wobbly and suddenly you've bought yourself a one-way ticket to fantasy land. A healthy way to channel these feelings is through masturbation.

For a long time, masturbation was only really talked about with regard to men, as if the rest of the population were far too prudish to get their rocks off on their own. But it's safe to say that's far from true. While it's extremely common to joke about people masturbating all the time (watch some films and there's more jokes about teenage boys masturbating than female speaking parts), masturbation for anyone with a vagina is often glossed over or ignored completely. It's thought of as something shameful or embarrassing that shouldn't be talked about openly. **But no more!**

I've been wanking all night. I ate four packets of crumpets and I think my clit might drop off. But I know exactly what I want.
AIMEE

Some people may not enjoy masturbating, or may simply choose not to and that's completely fine – it's all about personal choice. But if masturbation floats your boat, then it's important to know it's for anyone and everyone, no matter your age or gender.

Self-exploration gives you a chance to find out what you do, and don't, enjoy and can give you the confidence to ask for what you want when it comes to intimacy with a partner. After all, if you don't know what you like, how can you ask for it? Besides, if you're feeling horny you can always count on yourself to be there for that helping hand (or two, if the situation calls for it).

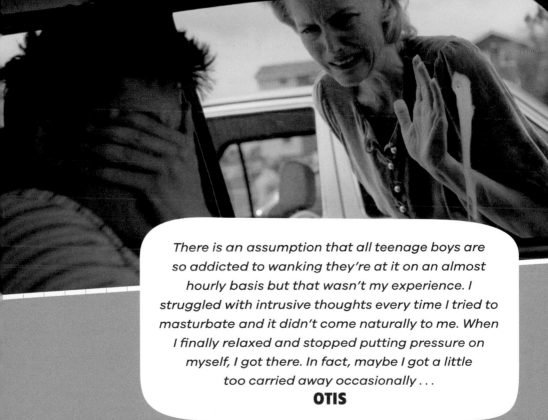

There is an assumption that all teenage boys are so addicted to wanking they're at it on an almost hourly basis but that wasn't my experience. I struggled with intrusive thoughts every time I tried to masturbate and it didn't come naturally to me. When I finally relaxed and stopped putting pressure on myself, I got there. In fact, maybe I got a little too carried away occasionally . . .
OTIS

THE **FIRST TIME**

When it comes to first sexual experiences, whether your very first time or first time with someone new, there's no one size fits all. But here are a few things to think about.

Some people spend years thinking about their sexual debut (it's never good to put too much pressure on anything), while for others it can be a total spur of the moment thing. It doesn't matter how it happens, as long as it feels right for you.

If you experience any pain or discomfort (the first time or any time), stop, pause or change what you're doing. If you have a vagina and feel pain but do want to be penetrated, you may need to reach a higher level of arousal or use some lube to reduce friction. Unintentional pain shouldn't be part of sex at any time.

It's probably not going to be like the sex you've seen in films or on TV. At all. Not just yet, anyway. Practice makes perfect!

You need to use protection. You can get pregnant the first time, and if your partner has been sexually active before, there is always a danger of catching an STI. The next two chapters will tell you all you need to know when it comes to contraception and STIs.

SEX ISN'T **ONE SIZE FITS ALL**

There is no one right or wrong way to have sex or enjoy sexual experiences. As with anything in life, it's all down to the individuals – what works for one couple might not be possible or enjoyable for another.

It's important to consider the needs and abilities of both people when it comes to sex. If someone has a disability or different needs, you shouldn't assume they can't, or don't want to, have sex. It may just be a case of tailoring the experience and taking into account any special requirements to suit both of you.

Sex is all about communication and mutual respect no matter who you are getting down and dirty with, so if you have any questions about how any form of sexual experience might work, it's always best to voice them upfront. Having an open dialogue will allow you both to enjoy any experience.

If you have any particular concerns around sexual function or limitations, you can always speak to a doctor for some advice. And remember that any form of sexual contact brings with it risk of STIs and potentially pregnancy,

so rubber up.

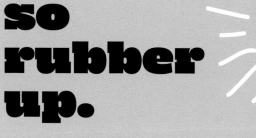

ALL ABOUT **PLEASURE**

Any kind of sexual experience should be about pleasure. And when it comes to sharing experiences with someone else, the only way your partner is going to know what you want, or don't want, is if you speak up and tell them.

It may feel a bit embarrassing to voice this to begin with, but once you've done it a few times it will come much more naturally and you'll hopefully be cruising down the pleasure highway with a massive grin on your face.

It goes without saying that it's just as important to do the same for your partner. Ask what gets them off and experiment. You may both fumble a bit to start with and no one ever gets it right every time, but that's all part of the fun. It can take a while to get to know somebody's body well, but once you know, you know!

If sex is working well between two people, you should both be having a great time. If only one of you is getting off time after time, something's amiss. Remember, sex is about mutual pleasure. That doesn't mean that you have to orgasm with every sexual experience; as long as you're enjoying it that's all that matters. But it shouldn't be about one person peaking and then simply hoping the other one follows suit.

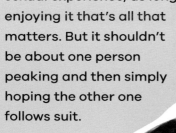

Sex isn't always perfect and it should be about feeling good, not looking good.
OTIS

SEXUAL **FANTASIES**

The source of all knowledge, Wikipedia, describes sexual fantasies as, **"a mental image or pattern of thought that stirs a person's sexuality and can create or enhance sexual arousal."**

Or, to put it another way, dirty thoughts and great jerking off material.

If you have them, know sexual fantasies are normal, healthy and can be very enjoyable, even if the subject matter does sometimes take you by surprise. One day you're bored as your brother's weird friend tells you how continents shift at around the same rate as your fingernails grow (true story), then the next day – wham! – you're imagining seducing them.

Don't panic, it's all OK. The chances are you're not in love with them, but forbidden love is sexy, and you know your brother would kill you if you so much as breathed near them.

People often fill their sexual fantasies with thoughts of things they would never dream of doing in real life (though never say never and all that). From dressing up to role playing, anything goes, and they're a great way of finding out what does and doesn't turn you on. So dream big, friends. Remember, if Otis can get an erection from looking at cheese, you can get your rocks off to almost anything.

According to Jean, there are hundreds of sexual fetishes, including ones you've probably never even considered, like . . .

ghosts.

All kinds of fantasies reign at Moordale, and although Eugene's penchant for medieval maidens may not be your cup of tea, if Viv's down with the idea then Alexa, play "Green Sleeves."

> *I'm very into nipple play.*
> **VIV**

While sexual fantasies can be a fun way to experiment, if the fantasy takes over, or both people aren't fully on board, it's important to say something and tell your partner how it makes you feel.

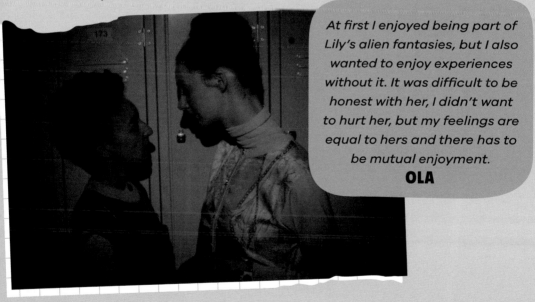

> *At first I enjoyed being part of Lily's alien fantasies, but I also wanted to enjoy experiences without it. It was difficult to be honest with her, I didn't want to hurt her, but my feelings are equal to hers and there has to be mutual enjoyment.*
> **OLA**

Remember, you never have to agree to anything that doesn't feel nice or enjoyable. Don't do anything just to keep someone else happy. But as for dressing up as a sexy ghost? Knock yourself **ooooooout!**

1 Masturbate in the shower. It's the perfect place for a bit of self-love. Just make sure you clean up after yourselves, please.

Last night I looked at some cheese and got an erection.
OTIS

2 **Try dry humping.**
No, I'm not taking the piss, it's currently very on trend. There's something very sexy about doing it, without actually doing it.

3 **Tell your other half what you enjoy.**
Your partner is not psychic, so you need to tell them what you like doing or having done to you if you really want to be satisfied in the sack.

4 **Don't worry if foreplay or sex isn't great every time.**
Sometimes it depends on yours or your partner's mood or the ambience. Sex doesn't always have to be wild and explosive so roll with the ups and downs.

5 **Always use protection.**
Keep away those pesky STIs.

ENTER THE WORLD OF SAFE SEX

Unless you're planning to start a family anytime soon, you need to be clued up about safer sex practices, i.e. all the different ways to prevent unplanned pregnancies and keep away any pesky sexually transmitted infections (STIs) – more on this laugh-a-minute topic in the next chapter.

When it comes to safe sex, there are no excuses: the protective world is your oyster. From condoms to coils, there are many ways to protect yourself and there's something to suit everyone. It's just a case of finding what works for you, and making sure you use it correctly.

Everyone who is sexually active (that includess any partnered activity) needs to use protection. Even if you aren't at risk of getting pregnant, it's absolutely the only way to protect yourself against STIs.

While safe sex at all ages is important, please also refer back to the previous chapter and the importance of the age of consent.

THE MIGHTY **CONDOM**

Back in the dark ages (the 1900s), if you wanted to have safe sex your choices were limited. You either:

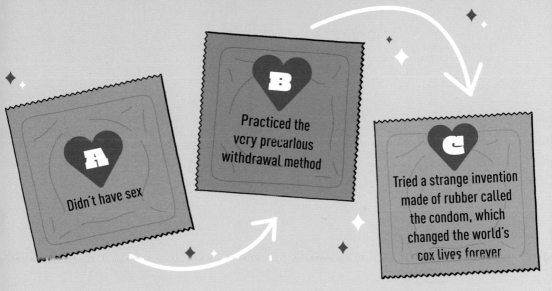

A Didn't have sex

B Practiced the very precarious withdrawal method

C Tried a strange invention made of rubber called the condom, which changed the world's cox lives forever

Traditionally it was down to the man to do the right thing and buy condoms, but it wasn't a case of walking into a pharmacy and perusing the shelves to find the right ones to suit the mood. It was, quite literally, one size fits all.

Often a gentleman would pick them up from his local barber, who would utter the cunning code words, "Something for the weekend, sir?" A swift exchange of money and the lucky chap could leave red-faced and sweating with his treasure safely squirrelled away in the inside pocket of his jacket (or maybe that only happens in black-and-white films?).

Until hormonal contraceptive for people with penises comes to fruition, the main option is condoms. But as they are the easiest way to protect against STIs, they are an essential.

At least there's plenty of choice these days:

LATEX

Latex is the material most commonly used
to make condoms because it's durable,
waterproof and stretchy. However, it can
cause adverse reactions in people with
latex allergies, which is why you can also buy . . .

LATEX-FREE

Latex-free condoms are usually made from a
material called polyisoprene. Some people use
them simply because they prefer the feel, so
consider branching out and giving them a try if
you want to change things up a bit.

TEXTURED

Textured condoms do exactly what they say on the box.
They have various surfaces – think ribs, dots and even studs
(thankfully not the painful silver kind you find on vintage biker
jackets) – designed to provide different sensations from your
usual garden variety smooth condoms.

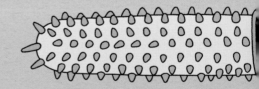

FLAVORED

Flavored condoms have become more popular in recent years,
and are often worn over the penis during oral sex as well as
during penetrative sex. But as some people can suffer allergic
reactions to them, it's always best to check the ingredients.

> *I am still horrified about how horrendous I looked when I had an extreme reaction to a strawberry-flavored condom when I was with Nick. My face blew up so much it looked like a bloody strawberry. Mor-ti-fying.*
> **ANWAR**

TOP TIP: always check the ingredients on the packet. Some flavored condoms use a sugar-based lube that can upset the PH balance of the vagina, and could potentially cause thrush, an itchy and uncomfortable yeast infection. Ouch.

LUBRICATED

As a general rule, all condoms come pre-lubricated. However, condoms that are labeled as lubricated come with extra lubrication, negating the need for the additional bottles/packets/tubes of lube, which some people opt to use.

WHAT IS LUBE?

Lube, or lubricant, to give it its full name, is a gel or liquid used to reduce potentially irritating friction during anal or vaginal sex. If having vaginal sex, always look for a lube that is labeled PH balanced. Water- and silicone-based lube is safe to use with latex condoms but oil-based lube can weaken latex so isn't recommended for use with condoms.

SIDE NOTE: if you're the type of person who finds it hard to make decisions, fear not, there are online quizzes available that will match you to your perfect sheath (yes, sheath is a truly dreadful word).

How do you put on a condom, you ask? Well, ask and you shall receive . . .

1
Check the expiration date on the condom.

2
Place the condom on the top of your/their erect penis. If you/they are uncircumcised, pull back the foreskin first.

3
Pinch the air out of the end of the condom. If you don't do this, it is more likely to burst during intercourse and is one of the main reasons condoms fail.

4
Unroll the condom all the way down to the bottom of the penis shaft.

5
After sex, hold the condom at the base while removing the penis to make sure it doesn't come off.

6
Carefully remove the condom and throw it into a trashcan (preferably wrapped in a tissue).

Remember that condoms aren't just the responsibility of those of you with a penis. If you have a uterus and are using another form of contraception to protect from pregnancy, it is important to be aware that one of the easiest ways to protect yourself from STIs is by using condoms.

Rule number one: enthusiasm is more important than technique.
ERIC

CHOICES, **CHOICES**

When it comes to protection for anyone with female reproductive parts, some might say they're spoiled for choice. But please bear in mind that aside from the internal condom, none of these methods of contraception protect against STIs. That cannot be stressed enough! Unless both of you have been tested and know for sure you're free from STIs, if you want to avoid a nasty infection, you need to double up.

THE COMBINED PILL

The combined pill contains artificial versions of the hormones progesterone and estrogen, and is generally referred to as simply "the pill" (a bit like a pop star that only needs one name). It works by preventing the release of an egg during ovulation, which means there's no egg for sperm to fertilize.

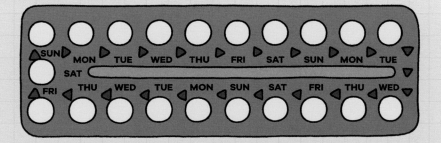

When taken correctly – usually at the same time every day for 21 days followed by a break for seven days – it is 99 percent effective, so it's little wonder it's one of the most popular forms of contraception in the world.

If you are sick, have diarrhea or miss a pill, the chances of getting pregnant are significantly raised. Early side effects of the pill can include breast tenderness, nausea, mood swings and headaches, but these usually settle down within a few months.

There are a number of different types of the pill available, so it's a good idea to talk it through with a doctor or healthcare professional to find out which one would suit you best.

PROGESTERONE-ONLY PILL

The progesterone-only pill, or POP, only contains one hormone (some inventive naming going on in the contraceptive world). It prevents pregnancy by thickening the mucus in the cervix to prevent sperm reaching an egg.

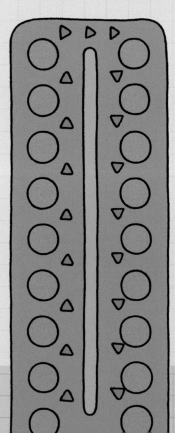

Like the combined pill, it needs to be taken at the same time each day for it be most effective, and may offer less protection if taken too late, or in the case of sickness or diarrhea. Unlike the combined pill, it is taken continuously with no break.

Side effects can include acne and boob tenderness, which should only last a few months, as well as lighter, irregular or more frequent periods.

CAPS AND DIAPHRAGMS

A cap or diaphragm is a dome-shaped contraption made of thin, soft silicone, inserted into the vagina pre-sex. It's known as a barrier method of contraception, and they are provided by your local healthcare facility, where a doctor or nurse will perform an examination so they can advise on the right size to use.

Caps and diaphragms work by covering the cervix so sperm can't make its way into the uterus to fertilize an egg. They are used alongside spermicides, often a cream or gel that contain a chemical to stop sperm from reaching its target (an egg). When used correctly it has a 92 to 95 percent chance of preventing pregnancy, although it needs to be left in for at least six hours post-sex. Diaphragms can be quite awkward and messy and can't be used during periods, but they are good for those who can't tolerate artificial hormones.

CONTRACEPTIVE INJECTION

The contraceptive injection releases progesterone into the bloodstream to prevent pregnancy. It is over 99 percent effective and can provide from eight to 13 weeks' worth of cover, depending on the brand.

Side effects can include headaches, mood swings, weight gain, boob tenderness and irregular bleeding, and it needs to be re-injected regularly to keep it working effectively.

CONTRACEPTIVE IMPLANT

The contraceptive implant is a small, flexible plastic rod that is inserted into the top of the arm. Incredibly, this tiny wonder steadily releases progesterone into the bloodstream to prevent pregnancy for up to three years. It may sound painful but it takes seconds to put in, most people only experience a little bit of soreness or bruising, and it is over 99 percent effective.

It's perfect for forgetful types who may not remember to take their pill, and it can be easily removed if it causes side effects, such as irregular, lighter, longer or heavier periods.

CONTRACEPTIVE PATCH

The contraceptive patch is a small, sticky patch that releases hormones through the skin and into the bloodstream to prevent pregnancy. It works in a similar way to the implant, but instead of going in your arm, you wear it like you would a band-aid.

The patch is changed weekly for three weeks, and you go patch-free for a week, during which time you have your period.

It can be worn in the shower, bath and swimming pool, and when used correctly it provides over 99 percent protection from pregnancies, and its effectiveness isn't impacted by sickness or diarrhea.

INTRAUTERINE SYSTEM (IUS)

An IUS is a small T-shaped device that is placed into the uterus by a doctor or nurse, where it releases progesterone. Depending on the brand, it can work for three to five years, is over 99 percent effective and is a great option for those who can't tolerate combined contraception, such as the pill.

It can feel uncomfortable when it's being fitted and there is a small risk of infection, so it's important to discuss with your doctor whether it's the right option for you.

Side effects can include mood swings, skin breakouts and boob tenderness but – wait for it – it makes periods shorter and lighter, and sometimes stops them altogether.

Hallelujah!

> *It wasn't f****** funny when I pushed you out of my vagina, either.*
> **JEAN**

INTRAUTERINE DEVICE (IUD)

An IUD, which is often referred to as the copper coil, is (like its close cousin the IUS) a small T-shaped device made out of plastic and copper that's put into your uterus by a nurse or doctor. It offers over 99 percent protection from pregnancy for five to ten years, depending on the type you have.

It's often suited to older people, but is also good for those who cannot tolerate synthetic hormones. Side effects can include heavier, longer and more painful periods for up to six months after the IUD is fitted, and there is also a small chance it could become displaced, meaning a doctor or nurse would have to perform an examination to check everything is still where it should be.

THE VAGINAL RING

The vaginal ring is a small, soft plastic ring that is inserted into the vagina and releases estrogen and progesterone into the bloodstream to prevent pregnancy.

One ring provides over 99 percent protection for a month, and it is not affected by sickness or diarrhea. Much like the pill, you leave it in for 21 days and then remove it for seven days, during which you'll have a period.

On the plus side, it may ease PMS and period bleeding can become lighter and less painful. On the downside, temporary side effects can include increased vaginal discharge, headaches and boob tenderness.

INTERNAL CONDOMS

Internal condoms are a barrier form of contraception made from soft, thin latex, or synthetic latex. They are worn inside the vagina to prevent sperm winging its way to the womb. Provided they are inserted correctly, they are 95 percent effective and – drum roll – they protect against STIs!

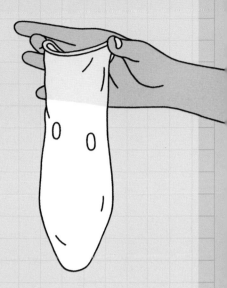

THE MORNING AFTER PILL

CAVEAT: the morning after pill shouldn't be thought of as a method of contraception, and should only be used in emergencies, for instance if a condom breaks or you forget to take your pill.

Depending on where you live, the morning after pill is available over the counter at pharmacies, and works by stopping or delaying the release of an egg (ovulation). You can take it up to three or five days (brands vary) after you have had unprotected sex, but the sooner the better.

> *Human boys are so fragile.*
> **LILY**

It can cause headaches, stomach ache and sickness, and if you are sick within a certain time of taking it (usually two to three hours), you will need to have another dose as you will no longer be protected from pregnancy.

The morning after pill doesn't protect you *after* you've taken it, so you will still need to use another form of protection.

After Otis and I had sex for the first time we couldn't find the condom. Nightmare. Otis is a good guy so came with me to get the morning after pill. He even offered to support me if I wanted to keep our potential baby. Can you imagine? I'm not going to have his pale, unusually long children.

RUBY

FERTILITY AWARENESS

The fertility awareness/natural family planning method is very dicey, but it's important for you to be fully informed.

The idea is that the menstrual cycle is monitored to give an idea of when pregnancy is most likely to occur. Protection, such as a diaphragm or condoms, can then be used during that time to prevent pregnancy.

As menstrual cycles can be affected by everything from stress to illness (as well as many cycles simply being irregular), it's an incredibly risky method of contraception, and not one to recommend.

THE WITHDRAWAL METHOD

The reason the withdrawal method (basically whipping the penis out of the vagina before you come) is not advisable if you're trying to avoid pregnancy is because there is a sneaky thing called the pre-ejaculate. It's designed to help with lubrication and it can get you pregnant. Avoid, avoid, avoid.

And use a condom.

IT'S YOUR **CHOICE**

If you try something and it doesn't feel right, doesn't appear to agree with your body, or you simply don't feel comfortable using it, always consult your doctor about other options.

Certain hormones work great for some people while they may cause negative reactions in others, so it may take a bit of trial and error to find out what works best for you.

You should never feel pressured into using – or not using – a certain type of contraception or protection by your partner. It's a personal choice and it's something you must feel totally comfortable with.

IF YOU DON'T FEEL PROTECTED, DON'T HAVE SEX. SIMPLE.

> *I belong to quick, futile moments of intense feeling. Yes, I belong to moments. Not to people.*
> **VIRGINIA WOOLF, A PASSIONATE APPRENTICE: THE EARLY JOURNALS, 1897-1909**

THE SECRET DIARY OF
MAEVE WILEY

If I catch anyone reading this, I *WILL* destroy you.

A FEMINIST: Someone who believes in social, political and economic equality for women.

WHAT IS FEMINISM? To me, it means standing up for what I believe in, being independent and wanting equal rights. At the end of the day, you would think that all women are feminists in at least some way, because surely no one is thinking "isn't it great that men get paid more than women for doing the same job?" If they are, they've got a screw loose.

Does letting a guy treat me nicely make me a bad feminist? Am I being weak because I really like feeling loved? Doesn't everyone want to be loved?

As long as I stay true to myself and never let anyone tell me what to do (as if), then why not let them treat me nicely. I deserve it.

> *Taught from their infancy that beauty is woman's sceptre, the mind shapes itself to the body, and roaming round its gilt cage, only seeks to adorn its prison.*
> **MARY WOLLSTONECRAFT, A VINDICATION OF THE RIGHTS OF WOMAN**

> *I* always *deserve the best treatment, because I never put up with any other.*
> **EMMA WOODHOUSE, EMMA BY JANE AUSTIN**

Some idiot bloke told me I was an "angry feminist" the other day. Why it is OK for men to have an opinion, but when a woman does the same, she's angry? Like being a feminist is a bad thing anyway? Putting negative labels around the word is the patriarchy's way of trying to keep women down and stop them standing up for what they believe in. I refuse to be put in a box because of someone's small-minded attitude. I'll always shout from the rooftops about equality.

Steve asked me the other day if men can be feminists. *OF COURSE!* One of the things I really like about Otis is how much he respects women and would never think for a second he's somehow "better" because he's male. I reckon that's down to being brought up by an amazingly strong mother like Jean.

MALE FEMINIST

My mum has had a hard life and made some bad choices. I've had to stand on my own two feet from a young age, but it's made me who I am. And I like who I am. I have never belonged to anyone apart from myself, and I never will. Thank god I had Virginia Woolf to teach me that when I was growing up.

7

THE LOW DOWN ON STIs (BE PREPARED)

There are numerous STIs (sexually transmitted infections) up for grabs. Some are quite well known but others you've probably never heard of. So jump in and get clued up on the worst kind of present around.

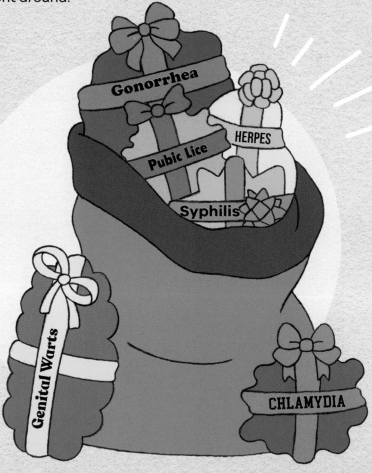

THE GOOD, THE BAD AND THE UGLY (HEADS UP, THERE IS NO GOOD)

What's the difference between an **STI** and an **STD**?

- An **STI** is an infection
- An **STD** is a sexually transmitted disease

Many STDs begin life as an STI, and morph into an STD.

BACTERIAL INFECTIONS are curable with treatment, while viruses often *can't* be cured. However, it is possible to catch bacterial infections more than once, even after you've received treatment and are bacteria-free.

STIs and **STDS** are spread during oral, anal or vaginal sex without a condom, and can also be passed from person to person via shared sex toys. It's estimated that over a million people worldwide catch an STI *every single day*.

If left untreated, STIs and STDs can cause everything from infertility to liver disease and in extreme cases they can be fatal. As the majority of people don't display obvious symptoms, they can easily be passed on to sexual partner(s) without either party realizing. That's why it's really important to get tested regularly if you are sexually active, and *especially* if you suspect someone you've slept with may have an STI.

It's important not to feel ashamed or embarrassed if you think you may have contracted something. No one is going to judge you – healthcare professionals deal with the same problems day in, day out, so be as open and honest as you can. There is no shame in catching an STI, just get it figured out for your health.

THE **BIG HITTERS**

SYPHILIS

In many ways, syphilis is the king of the STIs, having allegedly felled a few in its time (most notably ladies' man and beheading fan, Henry VIII).

Who, me?

Syphilis is a bacterial infection and it looked to be making a dramatic comeback in the 2000s. While it's still pretty rare, it does account for about eleven percent of all STIs in the US. Which isn't terrible when you consider that the symptoms include:

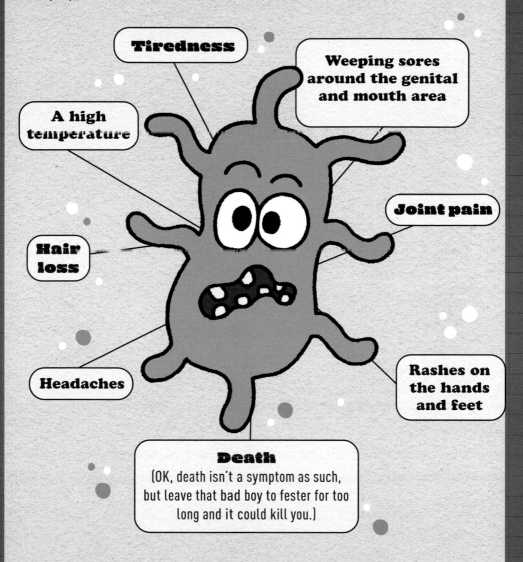

Tiredness

Weeping sores around the genital and mouth area

A high temperature

Joint pain

Hair loss

Headaches

Rashes on the hands and feet

Death
(OK, death isn't a symptom as such, but leave that bad boy to fester for too long and it could kill you.)

How is it treated? With antibiotics, and time is of the essence (see above).

(CHLAMYDIA)

When Moordale had a chlamydia outbreak, there were so many surgical face masks it looked like a practice run for COVID-19 (is it too soon for jokes?). But, in reality, it can only be caught via sexual contact.

I couldn't believe how crazy people were acting when Moordale had the chlamydia outbreak. It really showed how little sex education we get at school when people think you can catch chlamydia from the air!
OTIS

How is it treated? With antibiotics. If it's caught early and treated, chlamydia doesn't cause any long-term health issues. However, if it's left untreated, it can have serious health consequences for anyone with a uterus, causing pelvic inflammatory disease (a painful infection that affects the upper genital tract), infertility and ectopic pregnancy (where a fertilized egg implants itself in one of the fallopian tubes).

Meanwhile, if you've got a penis it can cause epididymo-orchitis, which is a very long and complicated word for painful, swollen testicles. But that's just step one. Epididymo-orchitis can also lead to testicular abscesses, where pus collects inside the testicles, or testicular atrophy, where the testicles shrink. Yikes.

CHLAMYDIA FACT: it's one of America's most popular STIs! Maybe "popular" is the wrong word?

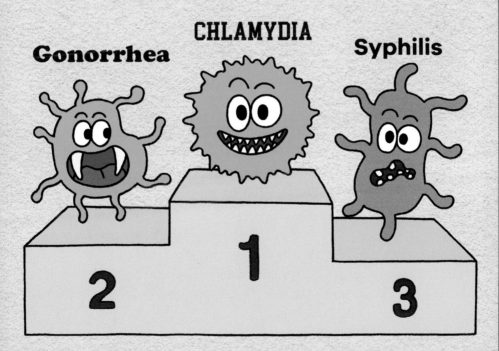

GENITAL WARTS

Yeah, it is as grim as it sounds. Genital warts, also sometimes known as anogenital warts, are caused by a virus known as the human papillomavirus, often shortened to HPV (probably because it's a bit snappier).

Symptoms include painless lumps or growths around your vagina, penis or anus, persistent itching or bleeding from your genitals or anus, or peeing a bit weirdly (sometimes warts can cause you to pee to the side).

How they are treated depends on what type you have, but treatments include a cream or liquid to apply to the warts for several weeks, freezing the warts off or, in more extreme cases, the warts may need to be cut, burned or lasered off. So swallow your embarrassment and get to a sexual health clinic as fast as your little legs can carry you.

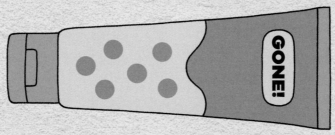

Just remember that the doctors or nurses you see will be dealing with cases like yours every day and there's nothing to be ashamed of. Don't let anything stop you from going for a check-up. It's always better to be safe than sorry.

While all of these treatments will rid you of the pesky lumps for a while, as genital warts are a viral infection there is no "cure" as such, so there's always a chance they may come back. The light at the end of the warty tunnel? Thankfully your body may well be able fight the virus over time.

HPV ISN'T JUST ABOUT WARTS, **YOU KNOW**

HPV (human papillomavirus) is the umbrella term for a very common group of viruses, most of which don't cause any problems. However, there are some known as the "high-risk" viruses that are linked to several types of cancer.

In some countries, young people are offered an HPV vaccine. A second dose needs to be given between six and 24 months later, and it is essential to have both doses to be fully protected. The vaccine protects against genital warts, as well as cancers caused by HPV.

Alongside vaccination, it's important for anyone who has a cervix to have regular cervical screening (also known as the far less appealing "pap smear"). The purpose of the screenings is to check for high-risk HPV cells.

During the screening a small sample of cells is taken from the cervix to be tested. If high-risk cells are found, they can then be treated before they get a chance to turn into cervical cancer.

It's important to start screening from your early twenties, or as soon as you start having partnered sex, whichever is earlier. As you can gather from the information above, it is crucial that you attend these appointments. The whole process takes a matter of minutes, but it genuinely saves lives.

GONORRHEA (AKA, THE CLAP)

Gonorrhea (the kind of word that could only describe an STI) is caused by the bacteria Neisseria gonorrheae, which sounds weirdly fancy, but it really isn't.

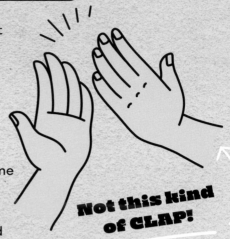

Not this kind of CLAP!

It's alleged it earned the nickname "the clap" back in the 1500s (it's something of a vintage STI) because men thought they could rid themselves of the disease by whacking their penis between their hands, or on a hard surface, in order to expel the pus and cure themselves. To be fair, antibiotics didn't exist back then, and they had to try *something* but definitely don't attempt this one at home.

Many people with gonorrhea don't have any symptoms but you should look out for the following:

If you have a PENIS:

- ◯ An increased need to pee

- ◯ Swelling or redness in the penis or testicles

- ◯ A thick green or yellow pus-like discharge from the penis

If you have a VAGINA:

- ◯ A thick green or yellow pus-like discharge from the vagina

- ◯ Bleeding in between periods (the above symptom will probably give you more of a clue though)

How is it treated? Your trusty friend, the antibiotic. Treatment usually consists of an antibiotic injection, followed by an antibiotic tablet.

HERPES

Genital herpes is caused by the herpes simplex virus (HSV) and is a lifelong condition that lies dormant in the nerves of the body. Because of this some people may experience repeated outbreaks although others might only have a few across their life or even just one. It is very contagious (i.e. easy to pass on) so it's essential that you keep yourself protected.

The main symptoms are pain when peeing, a tingling, itching or burning sensation around the penis or vagina, an unusual vaginal discharge and, the crème de la crème, small blisters around the genitals, anus, thighs and bottom, which burst into open sores.

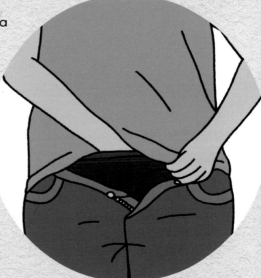

How is it treated?
Because there isn't a cure, sufferers have to wait for the symptoms to clear up, but antiviral medicine may be given to help speed up the process, and cream is often prescribed for the pain.

PUBIC LICE

Pubic lice, often referred to as crabs, aren't actually crabs at all. They are, in fact, small parasitic insects that are gray-yellow in color, about two millimeters in length and make a home for themselves in your coarse body hair (mainly pubic) where they live off your blood.

Pubic lice also lay eggs, which show up as brown dots attached to hair. As well as pubic hair, lice can attach to hairs on the legs, under arms, on the abdomen and chest and in beards. They also (rarely, but it does happen) attach themselves to eyebrows and eyelashes but they're not fussed about head hair, so they leave that alone. Why thanks, crabs.

Not surprisingly, the tiny multi-legged buggers cause extreme itching, especially at night when they all like to get together and chill with some tunes and a campfire (possibly).

Play Wonderwall!

How are they treated ? Thankfully you can buy treatment for pubic lice over the counter at pharmacies without a prescription. Just remember to hammer home the point that you're

"BUYING THEM FOR A FRIEND."

SIDE NOTE:
pubic lice make crap pets.

(Nothing like Madam!)

TRICHOMONIASIS

While we're on the subject of tiny parasites, allow us to introduce you to trichomoniasis, an STI caused by a tiny parasite called Trichomoniasis vaginalis (TV or trich for short). It is mostly found in the vagina, or the urethra in the penis.

Symptoms usually develop within a month of infection. However, worryingly, almost half of the people suffering with TV will not know they've got it, although they can still pass it along to other people.

Those who do suffer from symptoms can expect to experience a selection of these symptoms:

If you have a PENIS:

○ Needing to pee more often than usual

○ Pain during ejaculation and when peeing

○ Welling, redness and soreness around the foreskin and the head of the penis

○ A thin, white discharge

If you have a VAGINA:

○ An abnormal vaginal discharge that can be thin, thick or frothy, and yellowy-green in color

○ Soreness, itching and swelling around the vagina

○ Itchy inner thighs

○ An increase in discharge, which may emit an unpleasant fishy smell

○ Discomfort when peeing or having sex

How is it treated? Sadly there are no over-the-counter options for this one and a trip to your local sexual health clinic is essential. A doctor or nurse will do an examination of your genitals and a swab may be taken so

it can be tested in a laboratory. If your test comes back positive, it can be treated effectively with a five-to-seven-day course of antibiotics.

> *Intercourse can be wonderful, but it can also cause tremendous pain. And if you're not careful, sex can destroy lives.*
> **JEAN**

HIV/AIDS

There is often a lot of confusion about HIV and AIDS, so let's get things straight.

HIV is short for human immunodeficiency virus, an illness that damages the cells of a person's immune system, allowing everyday infections and diseases to thrive in their body.

AIDS stands for acquired immune deficiency syndrome, which is the name given to potentially life-threatening infections and illnesses that take hold when a person has not received treatment for HIV, and as a result their immune system has been severely damaged.

It's important to distinguish that AIDS cannot be passed from one human being to another, but HIV can.

When HIV first hit the news back in the 1980s, it was considered a death sentence. Because so little was known about the virus, apart from the fact that, devastatingly, people were dying from it, it caused widespread panic.

The public were so fearful, hysteria broke out and people began to believe they could catch HIV simply by touching or being in the same room as an infected person. Thankfully, society has come a hell of a long way since then.

While sexual contact is the most common way that HIV is spread, it can also be spread via shared needles, or if a person received medical treatment in a country that has low sterilization standards. It's also possible to pass it on to a baby while giving birth or breastfeeding.

Although some people will have no obvious symptoms, it is common for people to suffer from a flu-like illness for two to six weeks after they have been infected. Once those symptoms disappear they may not have any others for several years, but the virus will continue to damage the immune system, which is why it's crucial to get tested if you think there is any chance you could have been infected.

How is it treated? There is no cure for HIV and, *without* treatment, the average life expectancy after someone contracts the virus is nine to eleven years. However, highly effective treatments have been developed, meaning HIV can be controlled.

Medicines known as antiretroviral drugs or treatment work to stop the virus multiplying in the body, giving the immune system time to repair. With the right treatment, people can live long and healthy lives and reduce the risk of passing the virus on to others.

There are also two relatively new, revolutionary medications that are helping to reduce HIV rates by allowing HIV-negative people to use protective measures against the virus.

The first, a medication called **PrEP** (pre-exposure prophylaxis) is a tablet containing a combination of two drugs commonly used to treat HIV. They can be taken by HIV-negative people before sex to reduce the risk of infection, as PrEP blocks the virus if it does get into the body. PrEP can be taken in two different ways. A person can either take a daily tablet, or only when needed, in which case two tablets are taken two to 24 hours before sex, one tablet 24 hours after sex and another 48 hours after. In the US, you can get PrEP from your doctor or a sexual health clinic.

Meanwhile, **PEP** (post-exposure prophylaxis) is a tablet that can be taken after someone has potentially been exposed to HIV. It must be taken within 72 hours after the virus has entered the body and should ideally be taken within 24 hours. It must then be taken exactly as instructed for the following 28 days. However, it is not guaranteed to work and should only be used in an emergency, such as a condom failing during sex. In the US, PEP is usually available at sexual health clinics and a doctor's office. The key with PEP is to take it as soon as possible after potential exposure.

THE FINGER **WAGGING BIT**

If you suspect you may have an STI, it's imperative you get yourself to a clinic and get tested as soon as possible. And refrain from having any sexual contact in the meantime, to ensure you don't give the kind of gift absolutely *no one* wants to receive.

SURPRISE!

If you do get a positive result from your test(s), it's your duty to inform anyone you could possibly have passed it on to, so they can also get tested.

Don't let shame stop you from doing the right thing. STIs are just one of those things that can be an unpleasant by-product of being sexually active, and it's better to stop the spread as soon as you can.

If in doubt, check it out.

ERIC'S FASHION BIBLE

MORE IS MORE!

Gray is not my color!
Say what you like about Ruby,
she knows how to rock a look

FIND YOUR STYLE

Not everyone can pull off my look. It just can't be done. And can you imagine if Aimee and Maeve swapped clothes? Find a look that expresses who you are – because I'm sure you're fabulous, darling!

YOU DO YOU

Never let others tell you what's hot and what's not. When Ruby dressed Otis – I died.

WHAT'S TRENDING?

We're all influenced by trends and other people's style but don't be a fashion victim. Something that looks good on the catwalks of Milan won't have quite the same effect when you're queuing for the bus into town.

CLASHING IS COOL

I love it when clothes clash, especially mine. It makes it look like I haven't spent hours planning my outfits, even though I totally have.

SERVE EVERY DAY

Even if it's only a small splash of color, I always find a way to make every outfit I wear interesting.

DENIM IS MY DEFAULT

You cannot go wrong with denim. As long as your accessories are extra, denim is never dull.

BORED WITH YOUR LOOK? GLOW UP

Try a new hairstyle, go big with your earrings or buy an a-mazing bright lipstick. A makeover doesn't need to be extreme.

MY FAVE OUTFITS

1
2
3
4

8

LOVE IN THE DIGITAL AGE
(IT'S NOT *JUST* ABOUT PORN)

Back in your parents' day, they had to sneak a peek at a porn magazine if they wanted something to file in the spank bank. These days you can feast your eyeballs on orgies, fetishes and MUCH more via your phone in a matter of seconds. Welcome to the wild world of love and sex in the digital age.

THE PROBLEM **WITH PORN**

Porn is literally big business. Recent surveys and studies in the US show that . . .

40% of kids have received or sent a "sext" by age 13

64% of 13 to 24 year olds are actively looking for porn online

53% of 11 to 17 year olds have viewed porn online

One study showed that in the US . . .

84% of boys and

57% of girls have seen porn before their eighteenth birthday.

Watching porn from a young age has also been linked to higher levels of erectile dysfunction (an inability to get an erection) later on in life.

Even though it is classed as an "adult industry," as porn becomes more mainstream, increasing numbers of young people are accessing free websites, meaning teenage porn addiction is also on the rise.

This may come as a shock, but most online porn does not reflect real life. In fact, it's about as real as those cheap designer "Chanel" handbags you get on vacation.

That's not to say that all porn is bad. Some porn is made with the enjoyment of all parties involved and is about genuine pleasure. It can also offer people an opportunity to explore their fantasies or desires and find out what turns them on.

However, there is a lot of porn out there, much of which is extremely unrealistic so you need to be very careful about what you watch. It is easy for porn to create a huge amount of anxiety and worry, as well as forming massively unrealistic expectations around sex.

Here are some common themes that make porn problematic:

People are naturally hairless like Sphynx cats.

You have pubic hair for a reason. You have it on your genitals to protect against friction when you have sex, and it also helps to keep genitals warm. Grooming was covered in chapter three but it's worth repeating: there's no pressure to look any way.

All penises are huge (Adam is the exception rather than the rule and he feels uncomfortable about it).

Meanwhile, over in Porn Land, you'd be hard-pushed to see one that's under eight or nine inches (which is way above average – see chapter three!), so it's no wonder guys like Dex end up running around the school grounds naked after hiding out in the toilets to measure their junk.

Everyone has anal sex.

Anal sex is very common in porn but many people (both straight and gay) may never decide to try it. Don't feel pressure to do it because it's "just what sex involves," and as with all sexual experiences, make sure both parties are fully in agreement before you do anything.

If you decide you do want to try, bear in mind that anal sex can still transmit STIs and, because the anus doesn't provide natural lubrication, you will need to use condoms and lube to make things safe and comfortable.

Penises only look one way.

Some penises bend to the right, some bend to the left, some point down, some point towards the sky as if they're trying to spot Orion's Belt, and some are curved like a banana. Embrace your unique shape.

See also, labia.

As we touched upon in chapter three, there is no such thing as a good- or bad-looking labia. Everyone's look different and they are all beautiful.

> *Looking back, I can't believe I got myself in such a state about my labia looking "weird." When I watched porn all the women seemed to have such perfectly symmetrical downstairs areas, and I was worried my wonky lips made mine look ugly. It wasn't until I opened up about it to Jean, I realized porn stars often have surgery to make theirs look like that. What a faff! After having a good look with a hand mirror and admiring all its curves and crinkles, I learned to love my labia. I think they look like a luscious geranium. I even made labia cupcakes to encourage other people to love theirs too. Let's all love our labias!*
> **AIMEE**

All women have fake boobs.

They don't, and not everyone likes women with fake boobs!

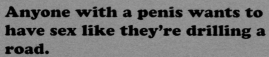

Anyone with a penis wants to have sex like they're drilling a road.

Sometimes a frantic quickie is just what the doctor ordered, but even the most rampant don't want to have sex like that all the time.

Women always orgasm.

Between embarrassment around sex as pleasure for women and not feeling confident to express their desires, sadly this isn't always the case. Many women need a bit more time to climax so the idea that they always come in three seconds flat gives an unrealistic expectation to everyone involved.

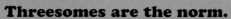

Threesomes are the norm.

Threesomes are so popular in the porniverse you could be forgiven for thinking you're boring because you haven't had one yet. If you want to give it a go and find two willing partners, that's great. But don't feel you need to put yourself into uncomfortable situations because it seems like everyone is at it.

You're not doing it right unless you do it in at least five different positions, one of which should technically be impossible.

Either porn bosses are hiring a hell of a lot of hyper-mobile actors, or they're not all that comfortable when their right leg is down the back of a sofa and their left leg is almost touching the ceiling. You do not have to contort yourself into unfathomable positions so you feel like you've given your session all you can. As long as it feels good, that's all that matters.

It's a good way to learn about sex.

It really isn't. A lot of porn shows unrealistic, and sometimes unhealthy, sexual experiences and you shouldn't be aiming to replicate what you see.

Just be aware.

If you do decide to watch porn there's nothing wrong with that; just be mindful of what you are watching. You can use porn to explore your sexuality, fantasies and desires, but keep in mind that porn is made for entertainment not as a documentary.

SEX**TING**

Sexting is sending sexually explicit messages, pictures or videos from your phone or electronic device. Here are some stats about teens and sexting from around the world:

In the UK, 38 percent of teens have received a sexually explicit message from someone else.

In the US, one in seven teens admits to sexting.

Sweden has the highest sexting rate in Europe, with almost 13 percent of eleven to sixteen year olds having sent images.

I tried sexting with Eugene . . . it didn't go quite to plan. Although once I was honest about what I was into, we came to a good compromise.
VIV

It's important here to note that under the current law in the US, it is **ILLEGAL** to share sexually explicit images of anyone under the age of eighteen.

That means that even if both people involved are under this age, it is against the law to send or receive the images.

Revenge porn, sharing explicit images without the consent of the person to cause them stress or embarrassment, is against the law in 46 US states, irrelevant of the victim's age. Therefore, anyone who uploads private, sexual images of another person without their consent can be prosecuted. Laws vary depending on where you live, please do research – it's always good to be informed of the laws around issues such as age of consent and sexting.

Safe cat pics!

In order for you to be fully informed, here are some useful things to think about if you are going to participate in sexting.

As with all forms of sexual interaction, it's important that everyone involved makes their own choice about when, how and if they want to take part in sexting.

Referencing back to chapter five, it's all about consent. If you do decide you'd like to share images, talk to the other person. What are you comfortable sharing? What are your boundaries? But there should be no pressure on anyone to send or receive explicit images and it's important to respect people's decisions either way.

If you are going to send images, think carefully about how much you trust the recipient as the images will no longer be in your control. The internet is amazing in so many ways, but once something is out there, it's very difficult to remove.

As with any relationship, sexting is based on trust. If someone shares an image with you, it is for you and you alone, and sharing it without consent is a violation of that trust. That still applies if you have an argument, are angry or break up.

If you find yourself in a situation where your messages or images have been shared, it can be overwhelming and upsetting. If you feel able, ask for support from friends, family or a trusted adult. If you would like, you can report it to the police.

> When the photo of my vulva spread around school I couldn't believe that someone would violate my trust like that. Everyone at school was sharing the image and judging it, I couldn't let it get out that it was mine. It would be mortifying. Once I found out it was Olivia who shared the photo, I was livid. Being angry at someone is no excuse for sharing private images. Only after Olivia and other girls at school declared it was their vagina at the school assembly did I feel confident enough to say, "That's MY vagina!"
>
> **RUBY**

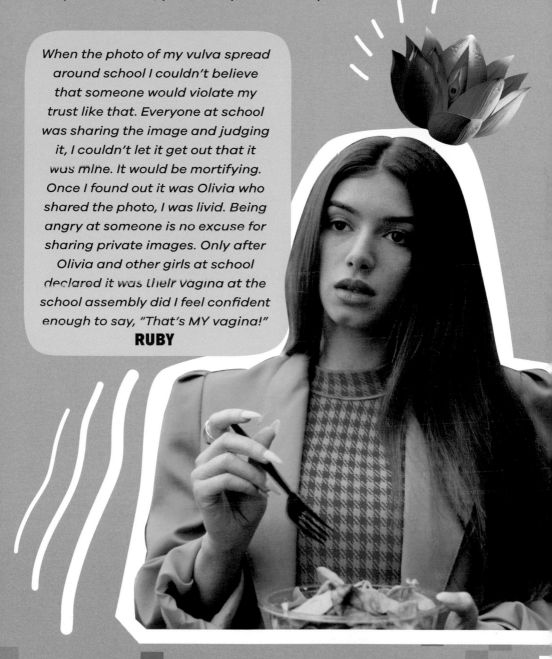

You put your trust in someone and they violated that trust; it can be a traumatic experience. It's a painful mistake to learn, but it is just a mistake. You are not a bad person and you do not deserve to be exposed or humiliated.

If you receive inappropriate images of another person, whether it be a friend, celebrity or a stranger, you don't have to look at them or share them further. Whoever the person is, they didn't mean for you to see the images. You have the choice not to cause further harm and violation of their privacy.

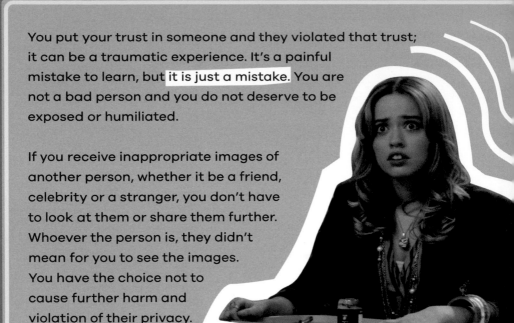

DO YOU REALLY KNOW **WHO YOU'RE TALKING TO?**

Online relationships can be a wonderful and positive thing. Chatting to potential new pals over the internet is a great way to make connections if you're shy, have limited mobility, have mental health issues or feel generally misunderstood or isolated. Finding an online community with shared interests and experiences offers so many opportunities.

However, it's easy to get catfished (led on) online, so it's always important to check who you're talking to is really who they say they are.

That gorgeous guy or girl you've been chatting to for weeks who has just started asking for suggestive snaps could easily be a sixty-year-old man who makes his fortune selling photos of semi-naked teens to dodgy websites.

It takes seconds for someone to set up a social media profile using someone else's photos, whether they pretend to be a celebrity or a civilian. If you get a DM from your favorite singer, your heart might start pounding, your head might turn to mush and you could soon find yourself doing things you promised you never would.

If you're concerned in any way, do your research. Look at their account. How long has it been going? How many followers do they have? Are people commenting on their posts? If in doubt, get a second opinion from a friend. And if you have any concerns at all,

BLOCK AND REPORT THEM.

MAEVE'S TOP TEN WAYS TO AVOID A DATE WITH **SOMEONE YOU'RE NOT INTO**

1 Be honest and tell them straight up that you're not interested.

2 Avoid all eye contact.

3 Block them on your phone and all social media.

MAEVE WAS HERE

4 If you're mates with them, go for the classic "I don't want to ruin our friendship" line.

5 If you're not mates with them, say you'd need to get to know them better before you can even consider a date, then avoid any form of conversation.

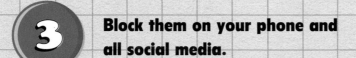

i don't do boyfriends

6 Say you're still in love with your ex.

7 Tell them you've got an STI.

8 Say you're not dating until a female President of the U.S.A. is elected.

9 Tell them you're only into people who can name twenty works of feminist literature.

10 Say you'd love to go on a date if they can get Bikini Kill tickets.

153

THE SERIOUS STUFF

Sometimes in life, bad things happen. It's a fact.

The world is an incredible, beautiful, mind-blowing place, but sadly we all have to overcome hard things and can find ourselves in nasty situations. If those things happen to be discrimination, harassment, violence, sexual assault, unplanned pregnancies or even rape, you need to be fully informed about what you can do.

UNPLANNED **PREGNANCY**

Sex shouldn't be a cause of worry – it's a fun and healthy part of life. But if you're able to get pregnant and not ready to be a parent, it's important to take all the precautions possible. We've outlined the different types of protection in chapter six and have potentially banged on about safe sex a little *too* much. But it is incredibly important to safeguard yourself.

Amazingly,

45%

of pregnancies and one-third of births among all ages worldwide are unplanned.

When it comes to teen pregnancies, around

50%

end in abortion.

Although, the good news is that there has been a decrease in unplanned pregnancies in the US in recent decades, and the number of teenage conceptions has decreased by 7% in recent years.

WHAT TO DO IF YOU THINK YOU **MAY BE PREGNANT**

If you suspect you may be pregnant, the first thing you need to do is take a test, which you can buy online and at pharmacies. If you get a positive result, you need to think really carefully about your next steps and what will be best for you.

This is going to be one of the biggest, if not *the* biggest, decision of your life, so it's important you don't rush into it. If you feel able to, talk to your parents, another family member, a friend or anyone you can trust and feel comfortable with.

Sometimes just talking things through can really help in decision making.

If you would rather talk to a health professional, you are able to get confidential advice from a doctor or nurse. Whatever you say will stay completely between you, and they will not pass information on to anyone else.

Of course, some unplanned pregnancies, although a surprise, end up being a happy accident. If you feel you are in a good position, emotionally and financially, and have the support you need to raise a child, you may choose to continue with the pregnancy.

If you decide you want to keep your baby, the next step will be a referral for prenatal care (which is also referred to as maternity or pregnancy care), where you will be guided and supported throughout your pregnancy by health professionals. You can get a referral via your doctor or in some places you can self-refer, and this should be done as soon as possible after discovering you are pregnant.

WHAT ARE MY **OPTIONS?**

Of course choosing to keep the baby isn't the right decision for everyone. If you decide not to keep the baby, there are a couple of options available to you.

ABORTION

If you decide you don't feel ready to have a child, an option that may be available to you is to terminate the pregnancy by having an abortion.

Terminations are either done surgically or via medicines. Abortions are safer the earlier they're done, and the majority of abortions in the US are carried out before fourteen weeks. It is rare for an abortion to be allowed to take place after that time, and it would require extreme circumstances, such as the mother's life being at risk.

Laws around abortion vary widely depending on where you live. If you are considering abortion as an option, please find a trusted source online, or speak to a friend or healthcare professional for advice.

Whatever you decide, remember abortions should only ever be carried out by a licensed clinic. Any unlicensed procedures are incredibly dangerous and, sadly, can result in death.

The experience can be difficult and emotional for a lot of people. If you can, it's always best to confide in someone you trust and have them accompany you for support.

> *Nothing says, "Happy Abortion!" like a bouquet.*
> **MAEVE**

ADOPTION

If abortion isn't an option for you, you can consider placing the child for adoption. For some this may feel like the right choice.

In order to give a child up for adoption you have to carry the baby to term and then give birth, so this is something you need to carefully consider. Are you ready and able to be pregnant for nine months? You also have to consider the emotional toll that giving birth and then placing your baby for adoption may have on you. It can be a very traumatic experience.

If you think adoption is the best thing for you, carefully research adoption agencies in your area. You want to feel comfortable with anyone that you will be working closely with to process the adoption. And remember that once the adoption order is in place, the adopter(s) become the child's legal parent(s), and the birth mother no longer has any legal rights over the child, so it is not a decision to be taken lightly.

As with all of these decisions, it's crucial you seek support from those closest to you or professionals when you need it. If you are in any doubt and need some support or advice from an expert, you can get this via hospital social workers.

Whatever you decide to do, you will need a huge amount of love and help from those around you, so don't ever be afraid to reach out if you're feeling overwhelmed or upset. If you would rather speak to someone outside of your family and friendship circle, you can always ask your doctor to refer you for counseling, or approach organizations for support.

SUPPORT

SEXUAL ASSAULT AND **RAPE**

As discussed in chapter five, it is essential that both parties consent to any, and all, sexual activity. Anything sexual you do with another person has to be by mutual agreement and anything that happens outside of those parameters is either sexual assault or rape.

In the US, sexual assault is any nonconsensual sexual act, including when the victim lacks capacity to consent. It also covers if a person is touched sexually without their consent. Sexual penetration is when a person penetrates the vagina or anus of another person with any body part or object, or oral penetration by a part of a person's body, without their consent.

Rape is when a person uses their penis without consent to penetrate the vagina, mouth or anus of another person.

If you are a victim of sexual assault or rape, it's not your fault. **End stop**. It doesn't matter whether you know the person, whether they are a complete stranger, if you were drinking or had taken drugs, or what you were wearing – the only one responsible is the person committing the assault.

If you are a victim of rape, you may feel traumatized, embarrassed or ashamed. These feelings are very common; you have been through a traumatic event and it will take time to process your feelings. As a survivor of sexual assault it's important to regain a sense of control over your own body and decisions so however you want to react is right for you.

If you have any concerns over injuries, STIs or pregnancy, you can get support from medical professionals as soon as you need to. Medical staff at hospitals, sexual health clinics or special sexual assault clinics are there to look after you and will do everything they can to make you feel safe and cared for. They will also be able to provide information about ongoing care for your physical or mental health.

There are also organizations that offer help and support for sexual assault survivors, so please check what is available in your local area. You can also look online, where you will be able to connect with people who are specially trained in this area and can advise and support you.

> *When I was sexually assaulted on the bus, I was so shocked I didn't really acknowledge the seriousness of what had happened. I felt embarrassed by the whole thing and that it was somehow my fault. Even after Maeve persuaded me to report it to the police, I didn't take it that seriously. But then I started to feel anxious taking the bus and became ashamed and uncomfortable with my body. It was only after I confided in Jean during my therapy sessions that I was able to begin to heal.*
> **AIMEE**

If you decide you want to contact the police to report the incident, a forensic medical examination should take place as soon as possible. It is also important that you do not wash the clothes you were wearing during the attack so they can be checked for forensic evidence. Reporting to the police will involve you having to retell events of the assault, which may be very difficult. If you have suffered any kind of traumatic event, try to speak to a trusted family member, friend or professional who can support you through the process.

SUPPORT

It's a fine balance, listening to people without inserting yourself into their reality.
JEAN

DISCRIMINATION AND **ASSAULT**

The importance of equity for all, understanding and accepting people for who they are, is an issue that is being discussed more and more. But there is still widespread discrimination towards people based on gender identity, sexuality, ethnicity, disability and religion. Bullying, harassment and verbal abuse are all forms of discrimination but intolerances can also spill over into acts of violence or physical assault.

> *I don't like to talk about it much, but I know that being an openly gay Black man puts me at greater risk of discrimination and assault. I experienced a hate crime first-hand and it completely changed the way I thought about expressing myself. I felt I had to make myself smaller and fit in with everyone else to not put myself at risk. In the end I realized that in order to be happy I have to live my truth, but it's something I have to think about every day when I'm just trying to be me.*
> **ERIC**

If you are a victim of assault, it can have long-term effects on your self-esteem, identity and mental health. If you feel you can, confide in friends or family, seek out a support group or speak to a professional who will be able to help you deal with your feelings. Many countries have laws protecting people from hate crimes so you can report any instances to the police if you feel able.

If you see any instances of discrimination, it's important to call it out however small it may seem to you. What someone may say is "just a joke" is prejudice and has no place in a fair and equal society. There are plenty of ways you can help fight discrimination including promoting the rights of all groups, increasing awareness, campaigning, educating yourself and those around you, and financially supporting nonprofit organizations who work to tackle injustice.

THERE IS SO MUCH
HELP AVAILABLE

Any kind of assault is a horrific thing for a person to go through and may take a long time to get over. There are many options if you feel like you need to speak to someone, including your doctor, who may be able to refer you for some counseling.

Please DON'T feel like you're ever alone.

HELP – I can't say no!

Whenever my friends ask me anything, I just can't say no. If they ask me for help with their homework, I do it for them. If they ask me to drive them somewhere, I'm playing taxi driver all night. I want to say no, but I'm worried they won't like me any more. What should I do?

Aimee

I always say that it's nice to be nice. If someone asks you for a favor, why not help them out? I know sometimes people might take the mickey a bit, like the time I had a party and loads of stuff got broken. But people just got a bit overexcited. I should have thought to move my parents' expensive things first.

But one thing I really don't like is people being mean – if someone's not treating you right, you have to respect yourself and know when to say enough is enough. But say it nicely – or maybe bake them a cake that says it?

VIV

Would you listen to yourself? I would never let anyone walk over me, and neither should you. We've got to look out for ourselves in this world – I know what I want and what I need to do to get it and if someone isn't bringing anything to the table, you don't need them in your life. This attitude may not make you the most popular person, but at least you, and everyone else, will know where they stand.

The main thing to remember is you have to respect yourself and your time. It's better to have a few good friends than spend your days sucking up to people who take advantage of you.

10

DEEP-DIVE INTO MENTAL HEALTH

From laughter to tears and love to hate, everyone has emotions that can fluctuate wildly from day to day (or even hour to hour, if you're having a bad day or someone is rubbing you the wrong way).

Being in touch with your emotions is really healthy, if painful at times, and the key to being more in control of them is understanding them better.

MENTAL **HEALTH**

Mental health is something that affects everyone. Even if you don't suffer with yours personally, it's likely you know someone who does, and the repercussions can be far reaching. There are constant reminders about how important it is to look after your physical health by doing regular exercise and eating healthy foods, but keeping your mind balanced is every bit as vital.

50% of all mental health problems in the US start by the age of fourteen, while

60% of young people with mental health problems in the US aren't being treated.

Mental health issues are nothing new, but in our grandparents' time, and maybe even our parents' era, they were brushed under the carpet and left to fester with the toast crumbs and a few rogue cornflakes. Thankfully these days people are able to have open, honest conversations about mental health and there are a huge number of resources at everyone's fingertips.

Partly thanks to social media and partly thanks to incredible mental health advocates, the old-fashioned stiff upper lip attitude is relaxing and the stigma is falling away. Finally,

IT'S OK NOT TO BE OK,

and to talk about it.

TALKING ALWAYS HELPS

You would be hard-pushed to find someone who hasn't felt their mental health wobble at some time, even if it's only short term. Everyone has a tipping point, and if external factors get too much, they can begin to manifest as anxiety, depression or other mental health issues.

There are so many things that can affect mental health, and everybody deals with them differently. An incident that some people will brush off easily can deeply affect someone else because it can trigger certain feelings. There isn't one perfect way to react to any situation, but the more you are aware of your mental health, and the ways in which it can be impacted, the easier it will be to understand and deal with.

EMOTIONS

Friends are supposed to listen to each other.
OTIS

Common situations that can challenge mental health include friendships, relationships, money, big life changes, decision making, health issues, sexuality, identity, body worries and traumatic events, such as death or illness of loved ones.

Research has shown that people with disabilities are around three times more likely to suffer from depression. Individual circumstances vary but it's common to feel more isolated from the world and it can be difficult to get the help that is needed.

Talking to people who are going through similar things as you can be a game changer. It can help you feel less alone and give you a different perspective on things. If you'd like to speak to someone, you can ask your doctor for a referral, look for support groups online or find a professional therapist.

Anxiety and depression are a part of everyday life for many. But how do they differ?

WHAT IS ANXIETY?

Everyone feels anxious sometimes in their life; it is a natural reaction to stressful situations. Everyone knows the sweaty palmed, butterflies-in-the-stomach feeling you get before having to speak in public or to take a test. Normally this feeling passes, but sometimes it can spill over into everyday life.

Feelings of worry, fear, unease or panic that linger for days can cause people to start avoiding certain anxiety triggering situations, making living a normal life difficult. Racing thoughts may make it hard to sleep, and sufferers often find it really difficult to relax or "escape" their thoughts.

There are lots of things you can do to ease feelings of anxiety and it may be that you need to try a few different ones until you find something that works for you.

> Identifying and keeping track of situations that make you feel anxious can help you see if there are any common themes that seem to affect you

> Allowing yourself set times every day to think about your worries

> Writing down your worries and then thinking of ways in which you can solve or challenge the thoughts

> Try relaxation, breathing exercises, yoga, mindfulness techniques – there are lots of useful apps that can help you to focus on the present and take your mind away from anxiety

> If your anxiety is badly affecting your daily life, or becoming overwhelming, seeking professional support may help

When people meet me they often think I'm pretty laid-back. But what they don't realize is that I suffer from bad anxiety because I can usually hide it pretty well. Having an open conversation with Jackson, and hearing about his feelings of anxiety, made me realize I'm not alone and I don't need to hide or bottle up my emotions.

CAL

WHAT IS DEPRESSION?

Everyone is probably guilty of saying, "I'm so depressed," when they feel sad or a bit down. But depression is feeling persistently sad for weeks or even months. Sufferers sometimes liken it to feeling like they're trapped under a heavy weight that they can't get out from under, or like being stuck in a dark room with no way out. Deep periods of depression can mean they can't see how things will get better, and they can experience dark, irrational thoughts or even thoughts of ending their life.

I'M ALWAYS SAD
- RUBY

Sometimes depression will be triggered by a specific event, such as trauma or bereavement, but often there is no one "cause." As well as feelings of unhappiness and hopelessness, depression can also manifest in physical symptoms of tiredness, insomnia, losing appetite, and aches and pain.

Everyone will experience depression in a different way, but the most important thing if you think you might be depressed is to seek help as soon as possible.

With treatment, it's possible to manage depression and even recover completely. Depending on the level of depression, treatments can involve talking therapies such as cognitive behavioral therapy (CBT), self-help groups, lifestyle changes or, in more severe cases, antidepressant medications

OTHER **MENTAL HEALTH ISSUES**

Anxiety and depression are just two of many conditions people can suffer from. If you feel like you may be suffering with any form of mental health condition, it's important to get help. Even if you've just noticed some early warning signs of any of the issues talked about below, please reach out. It's always better to get support before things escalate.

PANIC DISORDER
Panic disorder is an anxiety disorder. Sufferers experience sudden overwhelming feelings of anxiety or panic that they can't control. Often panic attacks don't appear to be linked to anything specific, and therefore they can kick in at any time.

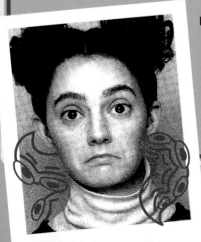

In many cases it won't be obvious that someone suffers from any mental health condition. Sometimes the people who look like they're most together on the outside are actually concealing underlying problems.

171

To everyone at school, I seemed to have life nailed. I was popular, seemingly happy, star of the swim team, girls fancied me. I never wanted to admit that I was suffering from anxiety because what did I have to worry about? But I suffered from such bad panic attacks, sometimes I thought I was going to die. Understanding some of the causes of my anxiety, and speaking more openly about it, has helped me get my panic attacks under control.

JACKSON

The fact that panic attacks can happen so unexpectedly adds to the sufferer's worry. They often become trapped in a cycle of feeling anxious about feeling anxious in case they experience a panic attack.

When I found out Jackson had hurt himself, I knew I had to do something as his friend. I went and spoke to his parents because he needed help.

VIV

Symptoms of panic attacks can include:

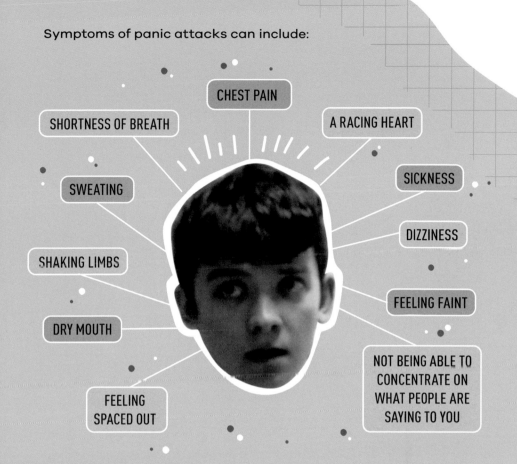

CHEST PAIN

SHORTNESS OF BREATH

A RACING HEART

SICKNESS

SWEATING

DIZZINESS

SHAKING LIMBS

FEELING FAINT

DRY MOUTH

NOT BEING ABLE TO CONCENTRATE ON WHAT PEOPLE ARE SAYING TO YOU

FEELING SPACED OUT

Panic attacks usually last from five to twenty minutes, but in severe cases they can continue for up to an hour. Some people may have several a week, while others can go for months without experiencing one.

It's important to stress that although panic attacks can be very frightening for sufferers or those around them, they aren't dangerous. The first port of call is your doctor, as panic disorder is one of the most treatable mental health issues. The doctor will speak to you about your experience and may do some tests to rule out anything that could be causing the symptoms, then refer you for treatment, which can include talking therapy or medication.

INSOMNIA

Insomnia is where you have trouble falling asleep, staying asleep or feel exhausted when you wake up despite thinking you have slept well.

It is very common to go through periods of insomnia (like those nights it's 4 a.m. and you can't stop thinking about who would win in a fight between a lion and a shark). But for some people symptoms can last for weeks, months or even years. A severe lack of sleep can cause loss of concentration, moodiness and, in serious cases, can lead to anxiety and depression.

Stress, worry, alcohol, caffeine, external noise and even an uncomfortable bed can all contribute to insomnia.

Insomnia can be helped hugely by practicing good sleep habits, such as:

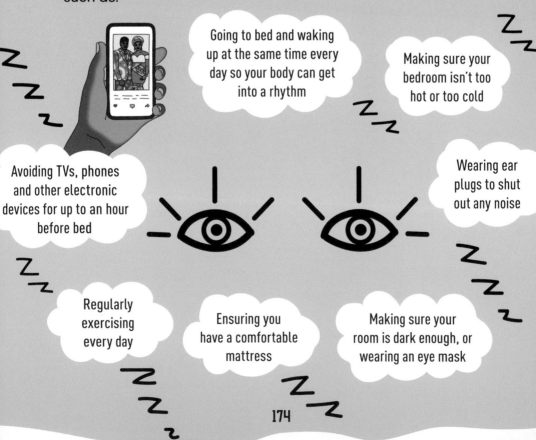

Going to bed and waking up at the same time every day so your body can get into a rhythm

Making sure your bedroom isn't too hot or too cold

Avoiding TVs, phones and other electronic devices for up to an hour before bed

Wearing ear plugs to shut out any noise

Regularly exercising every day

Ensuring you have a comfortable mattress

Making sure your room is dark enough, or wearing an eye mask

It is not advised to take over-the-counter sleeping aids as these won't treat insomnia and can have negative side effects. If none of the above tactics work, or a lack of sleep begins to have a negative impact on your daily life, you should speak to your doctor.

SELF-INJURY

Self-injury is when you intentionally physically injure or harm yourself. This can be as a way of dealing with overwhelming emotions, painful memories or trying to gain a feeling of control.

People often turn to self-injury thinking it is a way to numb their feelings temporarily. However, once the feeling of release passes, the emotions and distress return, making the sufferer feel worse and potentially causing repeat behavior. Emotional distress often leads someone to self-injuring – this can be from events they are currently experiencing or past traumas. Sometimes there is no obvious reason.

If you are already self-injuring, or if you have had thoughts about it, please seek urgent help from a doctor or a support organization.

BIPOLAR DISORDER

Bipolar disorder affects a person's moods – they experience huge changes in mood, from one extreme to the other.

Sufferers have periods of time where they have loads of energy and feel very happy and proactive; this is known as mania. This is then often followed by periods of depression where they feel sad, lethargic and hopeless. Some people may even experience thoughts of ending their life.

Unlike typical changes in mood, people with bipolar disorder can experience episodes that last weeks or more. It can be common for people to first be diagnosed with clinical depression as they may not experience a manic episode for years.

A combination of treatments can be offered to help people manage their moods. These include learning to recognize triggers and signs of a manic or depressive episode, talking therapies and medication. A doctor will advise the best course of action for each individual case.

Funfairs are simply a distraction from the inevitability of death.
MAEVE

OBSESSIVE-COMPULSIVE DISORDER (OCD)

OCD is a mental health issue where sufferers have obsessive thoughts and compulsive behaviors.

Obsessions are unwanted thoughts or urges that can't be controlled and constantly enter the mind of the sufferer. A compulsion is a repetitive behavior that is done to relieve obsessive thoughts. Sufferers may feel the need to compulsively repeat patterns to try and calm their thoughts, such as checking electrical devices are switched off or cleaning the same surface numerous times. Some people believe that if they don't repeat actions a number of times, something terrible could happen.

OCD can affect anyone, including young people, but it is more likely to develop in early adulthood. In extreme cases it can inhibit the sufferer's ability to lead a normal life, and professional help is needed.

As ever, your doctor is your first port of call, but there are also helplines, support groups and even apps to help with coping strategies if you feel your condition is mild.

EATING **DISORDERS**

Eating disorders are psychological illnesses that cause the sufferer to become preoccupied with their body and food, often due to emotional factors. Eating disorders are more common in women and girls, especially teenagers, but boys and men are also affected.

If you know or suspect you are suffering from an eating disorder, please speak to your doctor who can refer you for the relevant treatment.

The most prevalent eating disorders are:

BODY DYSMORPHIC DISORDER

Also known as body dysmorphia, people with this condition are often preoccupied with perceived flaws in their appearance that others often can't even see. Sufferers can become convinced they are unattractive, overweight or unworthy.

It has nothing to do with vanity and can have a huge effect on the sufferer's everyday life, to the point where they may feel too self-conscious to leave the house.

ANOREXIA

Anorexia, also known as anorexia nervosa, is a condition where the sufferer seriously limits or controls their food and drink consumption and can also exercise excessively in order to maintain an often dangerously low weight. They may also cut out certain foods completely and take laxatives to keep their weight down. A distorted view of their body means that even if they are ill and starving themselves, they still believe they are overweight.

BULIMIA

Bulimia, or bulimia nervosa, is a disorder where sufferers eat large amounts of food – known as binge eating. Then in order to compensate they will purge by making themselves sick or taking laxatives and diuretics. It is also common for people with bulimia to fast (not eat any food for a set period of time) or over-exercise to counteract the additional calories from binge eating.

BINGE-EATING DISORDER

People who suffer from a binge-eating disorder feel out of control with their eating. They may eat large quantities of food in a short period of time and feel unable to stop. Unlike people with bulimia, they will not make themselves sick after binges, but they may restrict their eating in between binges to try to control their weight. Binge eating is often associated with feelings of shame or guilt that can exacerbate disordered eating behaviors.

> *I might have said something about chinchillas giving blowjobs.*
> **OTIS**

DON'T SUFFER **IN SILENCE**

If you are suffering from any kind of mental health problem, please reach out, and never feel like you have to go through it alone. Whether you feel most comfortable seeking help from a professional or talking to a trusted friend or family member, there is *always* somewhere who cares.

BE MORE **OLA!**

Few people are as comfortable in their skin as Ola. She knows exactly who she is and never questions it.

Whether it's how she dresses (how cute is her sock style?) or how she connects with other people, she never feels the need to put on a front or try to impress other people. She isn't afraid to stand up for what she believes in or voice her opinion when she needs to, and, all in all, she's almost impossible not to like. So how can you be a bit more Ola?

1
There is a right way to have your say
Ola is incredible at having her say without bellowing or stamping her feet. If you want people to respect your opinion, it's important to state your case in a firm but calm manner.

2
Don't be afraid of your feelings
She gets angry with Otis and her dad sometimes drives her crazy, but Ola never apologizes for how she feels. She accepts her emotions and knows it's healthy to express them.

3
Be open-minded
When so many people wrote Adam off, Ola gave him a chance. She took the time to scratch the surface and look at what was hiding beneath, and they both discovered a great friend. Imagine if we could all do a bit more of that?

4
Don't try to impress

Ola couldn't care less about running with the cool crowd. She's super secure and if people like her, then great. And if they don't? She's totally "WHATEVER" about it.

5
Be yourself

Ola never feels the need to hide any part of herself or act out. She wakes up every morning and continues being her best self, which is her most authentic self. She is **100 percent** Ola.

11

A SHORT GUIDE TO HAPPINESS
(OR AT LEAST HELP YOU ON YOUR WAY)

It would be nice if you could simply buy a magic bean that would remove all your worries and make you happy. Unfortunately, it's not that easy. If it was, the owner of the bean shop would be very rich, and very happy.

There is no definitive guide to life. Everyone has their ups and downs, struggles and triumphs. Some days it feels like everything is right with the world while others it's hard to peel yourself out of bed. You can only do your best, learn from all of the experiences along the way and try to find happiness where you can.

LIFE'S UPS **AND DOWNS**

What a wonderful world it would be if everyone was wafting around feeling totally happy and at ease with themselves. But even people as gorgeous as Aimee or as funny and sweet as Otis have more hang-ups than a dry cleaner. An ill-advised comment here, a critical, overbearing parent there (hi, Adam), and your sense of self-worth is on the floor.

Sometimes life can feel like a constant game of

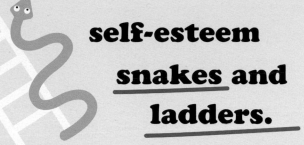

self-esteem
snakes and
ladders.

One minute you're climbing the ladder to Contented Town, and the next you're slipping down a giant snake and landing on your ass.

Everyone suffers on some level, whether it's a few low days here and there or more serious mental health issues, as covered in chapter ten. Some people face more difficulties or challenges than others, and everyone has times when they feel down, lonely, bored or angry. Humans have a myriad of emotions and no one can be in a good mood 24/7.

It's not always easy to feel good about yourself when it seems like the world wants to constantly knock you down. Sometimes happiness takes a conscious effort, and you have to look for joy where you can.

So here are ten tips to help you find a little happiness.

1 ONLY CARE ABOUT COMMENTS FROM THE PEOPLE THAT MATTER

Someone called you skanky as you walked past them on your way to the store. The first question you'll probably ask yourself is *why*? A casual slur can easily ruin your day, your week or even your month, and the likelihood is, you may never get answers. But before you start to question your hair/outfit/personal

hygiene, consider this: That person could be having a crappy day, could be really jealous of your amazing new sneakers, or they could have been daydreaming about their ex at the very moment you walked by.

The only people whose comments you should listen to are the people who truly know you, and that you care about. If someone is assuming something without even knowing you, the likelihood is they're a bit of a dick, so who cares what they think anyway?

DON'T BE A DICK

2 DITCH COMPARISON-ITIS

You may sometimes look at other people and envy what they have. But unless you stop comparing yourself to other people and feeling less than, you can never be truly happy.

Everyone is guilty of it. Even the biggest celebs compare themselves to other famous people, and probably cry under their Louis Vuitton blankets when a rival lands a TV or film role they were desperate for. Rejection sucks, no matter how successful you are. But even if you don't know it quite yet, you are good enough just the way you are.

3 DON'T BELIEVE THE HYPE

Everyone knows that everything on social media isn't real. If people are constantly having to tell you they're living their best lives via Instagram, you should ask yourself why.

Social media can unleash envy and tap into people's deepest insecurities, but the reality is that what you're seeing day in, day out is everyone's highlights reel. The chances are, no one's going to upload a picture of themselves being screamed at by their mom because they forgot to unload the dishwasher.

No matter how many followers and likes they have, they'll still be dealing with their own stuff, because no one is immune to everyday stresses. Pets die, friendships end, and those limited-edition sneakers they've been lusting after sell out in their size.

4 STAY CONNECTED

Research by lots of smart people shows that regular, in person connection with friends and family makes you feel better about yourself. Loneliness is nobody's friend (oh, the irony of that sentence), and being around the *right* people can give you a real boost.

Sometimes there's nothing quite like hiding under the covers with snacks and movies and having some self-indulgent me, me, me time. But there has to be a limit. If you start to find crumbs in your bed from food you don't recognize, it's time to join the real world again, and have a conversation with an actual person IRL.

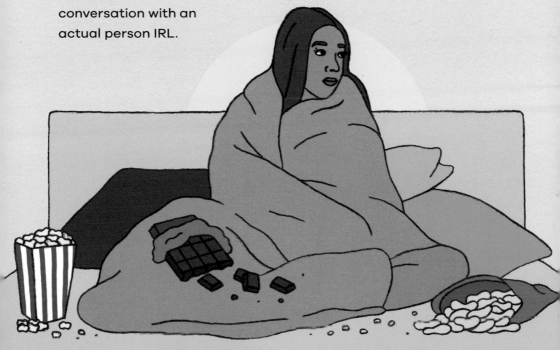

5 TELL YOUR NEGATIVE INNER VOICE TO SCRAM

You know that voice that is always telling you you're not good enough? That's your mean, self-sabotaging alter ego, and it's a downer. Sadly it's not one of those things that goes away on its own, so it needs challenging, and that can take a bit of work. One of the ways to do this is to give your negative inner voice a name, and every time it throws shade at you, tell it where to go.

> Hey, you're looking gross today. Is that a new zit on your forehead? You totally said the wrong thing when you bumped into James this morning. He's going to think you're such an idiot.

> Oh, shut up.

It may seem way too simplistic, but practice it enough times and it begins to work. Give your own negative voice less head space and it won't be able to keep putting you down.

It's time to **nip that negative talk in the bud.**

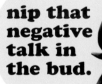

6 DO SOMETHING NICE FOR SOMEONE ELSE

When you're feeling really down on yourself, getting out of your own head by doing something kind for someone else can really shift things.

Even if it's just calling your friend who is having a hard time with their relationship and letting them spill for hours about

how they're doing everything right, and their partner is doing everything wrong.

It's really easy to get caught up in your own thoughts and misery and slip into "victim mode" without even realizing it. "Getting out of self," as expensive therapists call it, can help you stop obsessing about your own problems and look at the bigger picture. It doesn't mean you need to start stalking the streets for old ladies to help across the road, but maybe just thank someone for dinner tonight, even if the carrots are a little too al dente.

 7 ## DITCH HORRIBLE PEOPLE

If you have people who are negative in your life, you'll feel better if you don't see them. How's that for mind-blowing advice?

The biggest act of kindness you can do for yourself is to cut toxic people out. What's the point in you working really hard to be nice to yourself and feed yourself positive messages when someone comes along and ruins all your good work with one throwaway shady comment?

It's hard letting go of people, especially if you've been friends with them for a long time, but if you've given them a chance to step up and be nicer to you and they haven't taken the bait, they've gotta go. Read chapter one for more info on what makes a good, or bad, friend.

Would you keep a poster on your wall that says,

BY THE WAY, YOU'RE NOT GOOD ENOUGH!

No! So why keep people around who do the same?

 8 F OFF, FOMO

There will always be parties you're not invited to, or trips to the movies you have to miss due to family commitments, but tell FOMO to FO. If you went to every social event you'd never have quality time for yourself, so embrace JOMO – the joy of missing out.

Don't be afraid to turn invites down if you're not in the mood to go. There will always be other gatherings, lunches and football games. So if the idea doesn't float your boat, don't think you're a loser just because you would rather stay in and binge watch the newest reality series on Netflix.

EMBRACE YOUR BRILLIANCE

Stop ruminating on the things you're bad at and concentrate on the things you're good at. Not everyone can be good at everything. It's impossible!

You may be envious because your friend is super sporty and you don't even own a pair of running shoes, but they may wish they had your knack for making people laugh or your ability to be a good listener.

Everyone has their own personal skill set (if you're feeling really motived, stick a list of yours in your phone to refer back to). Concentrate on building on your many beneficial strengths and park your jealousy.

Sometimes when we learn new skills we can feel exposed.
OTIS

10 FIND WHAT LIGHTS YOU UP

That might sound basic AF, but honestly, finding what brings you joy is one of the simplest ways to make yourself happy. For Adam, it's training dogs. For Lily, it's writing stories about porno aliens. And for Maeve, it's reading books with a strong female lead.

Lazing in the sun and eating grilled cheese sandwiches may be great, but apparently doing that every day isn't (and you have to take rainy days into account), so find the things that ignite your passion. If there's nothing that springs to mind, try out some stuff! There are tons of great free online tutorials to find; look for a group to join or search out like-minded people to keep you motivated. And if you try a few new things and they don't work out, it's all good experience and you never know, you might get a good story or meet a new friend.

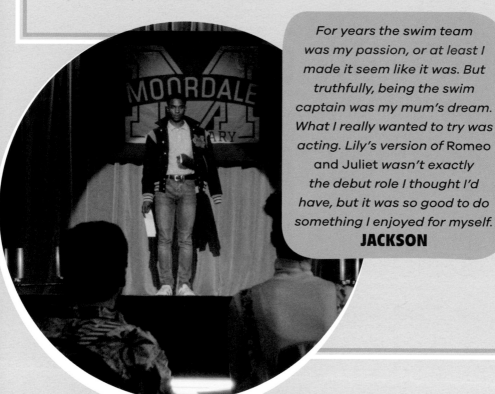

For years the swim team was my passion, or at least I made it seem like it was. But truthfully, being the swim captain was my mum's dream. What I really wanted to try was acting. Lily's version of Romeo and Juliet *wasn't exactly the debut role I thought I'd have, but it was so good to do something I enjoyed for myself.*
JACKSON

Don't feel you need to trap your hand underneath a set of very heavy weights, Jackson-style, to start trying new things. Whether it's writing poetry like Rahim, painting like Isaac, or taking a leaf out of Lily's erotic alien comics, there are so many new things to try in this life. Go forth, hobby ninjas, and . . .

THIS THING CALLED **LIFE**

> You are who you are.
> Don't let anyone take
> that away from you.
> **OTIS**

Life is a puzzle and you might often feel like you're missing some of the pieces. But whatever stage in life you may be at, always remember you are amazing.

Everyone is figuring things out as they go along and you're not always going to get things right. But if you surround yourself with people who love and care about you, try to be true to yourself and treat others with respect, you're on your way to a life well-lived.

RESOURCES

CENTER FOR YOUNG WOMEN'S HEALTH:
https://youngwomenshealth.org/

GIRLS HEALTH: https://www.girlshealth.gov/index.html

GO ASK ALICE!: https://goaskalice.columbia.edu/

PLANNED PARENTHOOD: https://www.plannedparenthood.org/learn/teens

YOUNG MEN'S HEALTH: https://youngmenshealthsite.org/

HELPLINES:

GET TESTED: 1-800-CDC-INFO or visit gettested.cdc.gov

LOVE IS RESPECT: 1-866-331-9474, text LOVEIS to 22522, or visit www.loveisrespect.org

NATIONAL SEXUAL ASSAULT HOTLINE: 800-656-HOPE (4673) or visit https://rainn.org

This book has been reviewed by experts, sex therapists and inclusion sensitivity readers including psychiatrist and author, Dr. Max Pemberton; certified sex educator and Doctor of Education, Dr. Nadine Thornhill; and mental health practitioner, educator and SRE facilitator, Charlie Hart.